MENSWEAR FASHION FORWARD DESIGNERS
Copyright ©2012 Instituto Monsa de Ediciones

Editor, concept and project director
Josep Maria Minguet

Art director, text, design and layout
Louis Bou Romero @ Monsa Publications

©2012 Instituto Monsa de Ediciones
Gravina, 43
08930 Sant Adrià del Besòs
Barcelona-Spain
Tel. +34 93 381 00 50
Fax +34 93 381 00 93

monsa@monsa.com
www.monsa.com

Visit our official online store!
www.monsashop.com

Follow us on facebook!
facebook.com/monsa.publications

ISBN: 978-84-15223-63-4

Depósito Legal: B-10902-2012

Printed in Spain by BIGSA

Cover photo courtesy of
George Bezhanishvili
Photography: Sidney Son
LeopardMilkshake Team

Endpapers, and page 9:
Julian Zigerli
Sugar, spice, and everything nice
Autumn Winter 2011
Photography: Ben Lamberty

Left 6:
Martin Lamothe
Park Life
Autumn Winter 2012-13
Photography: Biel Sol

La tipografía "NICO" ha sido diseñada por Ipsum Planet para la revista Neo2 (www.neo2.es)
NICO typography designed by psum Planet for Neo2 magazine (www.neo2.es)

MENSWEAR
*f*ASHION *f*ORWARD
DESIGNERS

selected by Louis Bou

monsa

BOYS WILL BE BOYS

On the pages of this book we will find an amazing selection of some of the best menswear fashion designers that are breaking the rules today, running away from the traditional codes involving men's fashion. In *Menswear Fashion Forward Designers* we will discover a new generation of avant-garde designers. What are the latest trends and styles? What is the future of fashion design for men? The designers show us, through stunning photographs, technical drawings and illustrations, how are their frenetic professional lives, how they work, and which are their dreams, the secrets behind their success, the aesthetic that shapes their designs, and why there is nothing prim nor proper about their creations. This is undoubtedly, the perfect book for students, fashion designers and fashionistas.

En las páginas de este libro descubriremos una cuidadosa selección de los diseñadores de moda masculina que actualmente están desbaratando las reglas, apartándose libremente de los códigos más tradicionales que etiquetan la moda para el hombre. En *Menswear Fashion Forward Designers* nos encontramos frente a una nueva generación de diseñadores vanguardistas que no conocen la palabra límite. ¿Cuáles son las últimas tendencias? ¿Cual es el futuro del diseño de moda para hombre? Los diseñadores nos muestran a través de magníficas fotografías e ilustraciones, como es su frenética vida profesional y como trabajan, desvelándonos los secretos detrás de sus creaciones. Este es, sin lugar a dudas, el libro perfecto para estudiantes, diseñadores de moda y fashion victims.

JULIAN ZIGERLI

www.julianzigerli.com
ZURICH
Switzerland

Julian Zigerli was born and raised in Switzerland. At the age of 20, he moved to Berlin to study fashion design at the Berlin University of the Arts. One of his professors, the fashion desginer Stephan Schneider, lead him through his studies. After graduating in 2010, Zigerli decided to return back to his roots in Switzerland, with the aim of working with the innovative swiss fabric industry. That is where and when he started his own men's fashion label.

Zigerli's main interest, besides taking care of his own brand, is making costumes for plays and movies. He has recently designed costumes for Wolfgang Bauer's play, *Magic Afternoon*, premiered at the Theater Neumarkt in Zurich.

Zigerli debuted, in 2011, with his first collection *Sugar, spice, and everything nice*. After that, with a lot of followers all around the globe, it was followed by the Spring Summer 2012 collection *Over stick and stone*. His innovative and loving-every-detail signature look sprawls from lichens and mutualism, to the strong, lonesome hiker and his journeys. A collection full of longings, which last beyond the mountains and canyons of the big city. Zigerli's men's collection stands for useful, smart and technical highclass pieces with a sporty touch. There is always a lot of love, color, humour and positivity involved in his designs.

Julian Zigerli nació y se crió en Suiza. Con tan solo 20 años, se traslada a Berlín para estudiar diseño de moda en la University of the Arts. Uno de sus profesores, el diseñador de moda Stephan Schneider, le guiará en su carrera de estudiante. En el 2010, después de graduarse, Zigerli decide retomar sus raíces y vuelve a Suiza con el objetivo de trabajar con la innovadora industria textil de ese país. En ese mismo instante decide crear su propia marca de ropa para hombres.

Uno de los principales intereses de Zigerli, además de encargarse de su propia marca, es el diseño de vestuario para obras de teatro y películas. Recientemente ha diseñado el vestuario para la obra de Wolfgang Bauer, *Magic Afternoon*, que se estrenó en el Theater Neumarkt en Zurich.

Zigerli debuta, en el año 2011, con su primera colección *Sugar, spice, and everything nice*. Poco después, tras el éxito de su debut y con una gran cantidad de seguidores en todo el mundo, decide lanzar su segunda colección primavera verano 2012 *Over stick and stone*. Una colección llena de prendas útiles, muy estudiadas e inteligentes, fabricadas con una calidad y una tecnología muy avanzadas, pero siempre con un toque deportivo. Todas las prendas que diseña Zigerli están impregnadas de mucha pasión, color, sentido del humor y positividad.

Page 10:
Julian Zigerli by Rico Scagliola
& Michael Meier

Page 11:
Over Stick And Stone
Spring Summer 2012
Photography: Amanda Camenisch

On these pages:
To Infinity And Beyond
Autumn Winter 2012
Photography: Amanda Camenisch

On these pages:
Over Stick And Stone
Spring Summer 2012
Photography: Amanda Camenisch

Page 13:
Over Stick And Stone
Spring Summer 2012
Photography: Amanda Camenisch

On these pages:
Julian Zigerli backstage
Over stick and stone
Spring Summer 2012
Photography: Rico Scagliola

On the following pages:
Over Stick And Stone
Spring Summer 2012
Photography: Amanda Camenisch

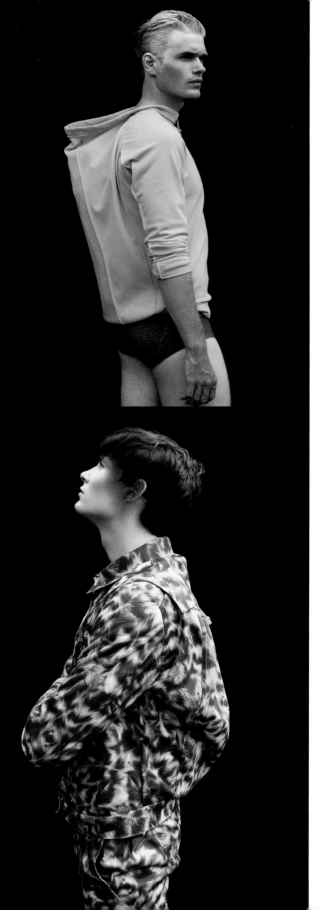

On these pages:
Sugar, spice, and everything nice
Autumn Winter 2011
Photography: Ben Lamberty
Technical drawings by Julian Zigerli

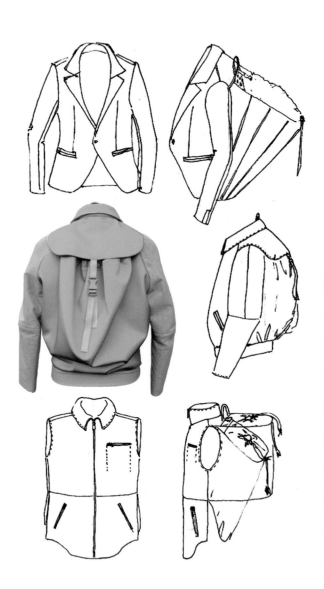

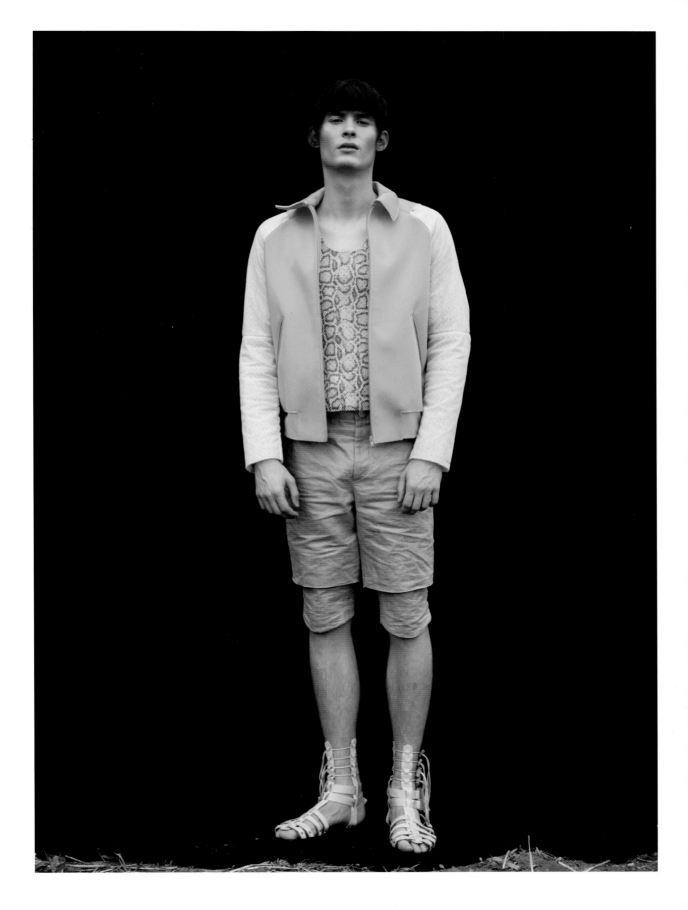

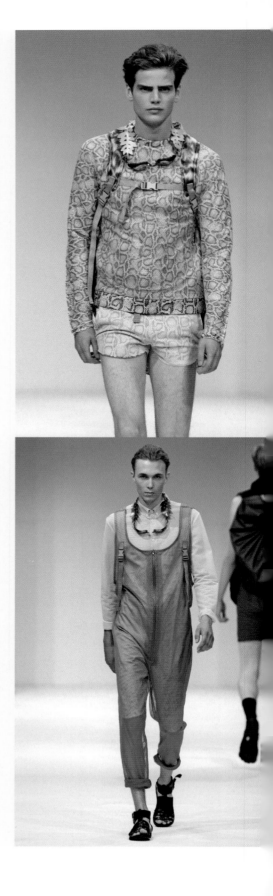

This page:
To Infinity And Beyond
Autumn Winter 2012

Left page:
Julian Zigerli on the catwalk
Sugar, spice, and everything nice
Autumn Winter 2011

CLAUDIA CAURIAND

claudiacauriand.com
PARIS

Claudia Cauriand decided to be a fashion designer a decade ago. Claudia have always been attracted to fashion world, her grandmother, a dressmaker, have influenced her a lot, always searching new fabrics in her vintage treasure, and learned from her how to sew and knit. Claudia decided to study fashion design at the Atelier Chardon Savard : Ecole de stylisme de mode in Paris. She graduated in 2001, specialized in knitting. This final year represent a turning point, because she discovered more about menswear while creating her own line. She tries everyday to fill her ideas to construct her own style with colorful prints and different fabrics, to mix them with different styles of clothing.

Water ranges and depths inspired her first menswear collection. On the surface, with random reflections of the sky, clear water displays different shades of blue, and deeper where a microscopic life reveals a combination of saturated colours, and organic graphics. When blue colour is more intense it refers to the loose and draped Tuareg silhouettes. We can spot some of the Tuareg dress codes in her collection such as djellabas, shirts, and oversized pants revisited into a urban spirit. The fluid and modern composition of these silhouettes, designed by Claudia, also stems from knitted pieces that are harmoniously draped. The summer materials like cotton and linen are broken in different heights and weights, sometimes transparent, and sometimes iridescent like the glittering light of the water surface.

Claudia Cauriand decidió ser diseñadora de moda hace más de una década. Claudia siempre se ha sentido irresistiblemente atraída hacia el mundo de la moda. Su primera influencia fue su abuela, que era modista, Claudia se pasaba el tiempo buscando tejidos en su tesoro *vintage*, y aprendió de ella a coser y a tejer. Estudió en el Atelier Chardon Savard : Ecole de stylisme de mode de la Mode, en París, donde se especializó en punto. Descubrió el mundo de la moda masculina mientras estaba diseñando su propia línea de mujer. Claudia intenta buscar su identidad usando estampados coloridos y buscando tejidos diferentes para mezclarlos con distintos estilos de ropa.

Su primera colección de hombre se inspiró en los diferentes tonos y profundidades del agua. En la superficie, con reflejos del cielo, el agua clara nos muestra diferentes tonos de azul, y en lo más profundo nos revela una vida microscópica, una combinación de colores saturados y gráficos orgánicos. Cuando el color azul es más intenso, hace referencia también a las siluetas sueltas y drapeadas de los Tuareg. Podemos encontrar estas referencias en la colección como por ejemplo chilabas, camisas y pantalones oversize, con un toque urbano. En la composición de estas siluetas también encontraremos algunas piezas tejidas encima de prendas drapeadas. Materiales de verano como el algodón o el lino que se combinan con tejidos transparentes e incluso iridiscentes como la luz brillante de la superficie del agua.

Page 24:
Claudia Cauriand
by Elodie Daguin

Page 25:
Out Of Colored Water
Spring Summer 2011 2012
Photography: Elodie Daguin

On these pages:
Out Of Colored Water
Spring Summer 2011 2012
Photography: Elodie Daguin
Illustrations by Claudia Cauriand

On these pages:
Out Of Colored Water
Spring Summer 2011 2012
Photography: Elodie Daguin
Illustrations by Claudia Cauriand

ZEM

zem-men.com
ROTTERDAM
The Netherlands

Samira Algoe is a fashion designer graduated at the Amsterdam Fashion Institute in 2010. During her studies Samira get a real interest for menswear clothing. After her graduation she decided to start her own label *ZEM*, to share her ideas and concept on menswear. The label is focused on the transformation of archetypical menswear from a more futuristic and fashion forward perspective. Old is new again. *ZEM* explores menswear fashion design looking for a new identity, breaking the boundaries to reach men's fragile side. A sincere devoted to graphic formalism, and structuralism, Samira finds from it a never-ending source of inspiration for shapes, colours and fabrics. She is also a minimalist lover so she pays attention on the more insignificant details to ensure high quality and wearable clothing for self-assured, and open-minded men who feel comfortable in their own skin.

Samira Algoe se graduó en el Fashion Institute de Amsterdam en 2010. Durante sus estudios Samira comezó a interesarse por la moda masculina. Después de su graduación, decidió comenzar su propia marca *ZEM*. La firma se centra en la transformación de los arquetipos de la moda masculina bajo una perspectiva más arriesgada y futurista. Lo viejo es nuevo otra vez. *ZEM* explora el diseño de la moda masculina en busca de una nueva identidad, rompiendo las barreras, para llegar al lado más frágil de los hombres. Amante del formalismo gráfico y del estructuralismo, Samira encuentra en ello una fuente inagotable de inspiración de formas, colores y tejidos. Minimalista y perfeccionista, le gusta prestar atención a los detalles más insignificantes para garantizar la calidad de su ropa, que diseña para hombres seguros de sí mismos, de mente abierta, que se sientan cómodos en su propia piel.

Page 30:
Samira Algoe by
Heleen van der Meer

Page 31:
Spring Summer 2012
Photography: Marco van Rijt

On these pages:
Spring Summer 2012
Photography: Marco van Rijt
and Peter Stigter

On these pages:
Spring Summer 2012
Photography: Marco van Rijt
and Peter Stigter
Illustrations by Samira Algoe

ANA LOCKING

www.analocking.com
MADRID
Spain

Ana González founded Locking Shocking in 1996 with a partner for 10 years, but they dissolved the brand in 2007. During those years Ana worked as creative director, winning the L'Oreal Paris Award in 2003, and the Grand Prix de la Moda from *Marie Claire* magazine for the best national designer in 2004. In 2008, Ana finally decided to start her new label Ana Locking. With her first collection titled *Reentry*, Ana won the L'Oreal Paris Award for the Pasarela Cibeles Madrid's best collection, during the Madrid fashion week. In September 2009 she presented her collection Spring Summer 2010 in the New York's Public Library during the New York's Fashion Week. In November 2009 she won the *Cosmopolitan* magazine prize for the best designer of the year.

Ana keeps herself updated to the latest new artistic disciplines, that's why she often collaborates with different cultural institutions and artistic organizations: from exhibitions to installations, video art, photography, seminars, and conferences. All of these projects make her grow up to evolve as the creative person she is.

Ana González funda en 1996 Locking Shocking junto a su socio, un tándem que durará solo una década ya que, en el 2007, la firma se disuelve. Durante esos años Ana ejerce la labor de directora creativa recibiendo el reconocimiento del público y de la crítica, además de galardones como el Premio L´Oreal Paris a la mejor colección o el Grand Prix de la moda de *Marie Claire* como mejor diseñador nacional en el 2004. En el 2008 crea su nueva marca, Ana Locking y la colección debut *Reentry* recibe el premio L´Oreal París a la mejor colección de la Pasarela Cibeles Madrid. En septiembre del 2009 presenta su colección primavera verano 2010 en la New York's Public Library durante la semana de la moda de Nueva York. En noviembre del 2009, *Cosmopolitan* le otorga el premio a la mejor diseñadora del año.

Ana mantiene fuertes lazos con otras disciplinas artísticas y colabora regularmente con diversas instituciones culturales y entidades artísticas, participando en exposiciones, instalaciones, video arte y fotografía. Ana también imparte seminarios, conferencias y cursos.

This page:
Under Beauty
Spring Summer 2012
Photography: Biel Sol
Illustration by Ana Locking

Righ page:
Under Beauty
Spring Summer 2012
Photography: Biel Sol

On these pages:
Antídoto
Spring Summer 2010
Photography: Biel Sol

This page:
Spinning Destiny
Autumn Winter 2010-11
Photography: Biel Sol
Illustration by Ana Locking

Right page:
Keep your stance
Autumn Winter 2011-12
Photography: Biel Sol

On these pages:
Insides
Spring Summer 2011
Photography: Biel Sol

ASHER LEVINE

asherlevine.com
NEW YORK CITY

Asher Levine, a boy out of Port Charlotte, Forida, arrived in New York to complete a degree in Managerial Entrepreneurship at Pace University, understanding that fashion, just like any other industry, is fundamentally a business. Shortly after graduating and with little over a decade of design experience, he started his eponymous label out of his basement in the West Village. It wasn't long before his luridly edgy menswear designs took root in the community. Consistent with his previous collections, his work wrecks havoc with the theme of organicism in fashion. The work, often heavily influenced by the natural world, not only flirts with the ideas of the visceral, but also, takes an explorative stance on the human figure and its condition. His seductive designs are in a constant state of flux between: fluidity and rigidity; beauty and disfigurement; abstraction and form; darkness and lightness.

As a result, his clothes often spectacularly engineered are just that, a spectacle, which in many ways have led him to attain both a cult-like underground following and a strong celebrity clientele with the likes of: Lady GaGa, The Black Eyed Peas, Bruno Mars, and the Scissor Sisters, just to name a few. However, it is this commercial line, originally dreamed about by a 10 year old boy, that is becoming the star and not merely due to his clientele.

Asher Levine, es un chico de Port Charlotte, Florida, que fue a Nueva York para completar su licenciatura en empresariales en la Pace University, comprendiendo que la moda, como cualquier otra industria, es fundamentalmente un negocio. Poco después de graduarse y con una década de experiencia en diseño, creó su propia marca en un sótano del West Village. No pasó mucho tiempo para que sus morbosos diseños para hombre echaran raíces en el mundillo. Fiel a sus colecciones anteriores, su trabajo destruye el caos del organicismo que existe en el mundo de la moda. Influenciado por la naturaleza, no solo flirtea con las vísceras, sino que explora la figura humana y su condición. Sus seductores diseños están en un estado constante de fluidez y rigidez, lo bello y lo deforme, la abstracción y la forma, la oscuridad y la luminosidad.

Como resultado de toda esta filosofía, sus prendas, de alta ingeniería, son sólo eso, un espectáculo en sí mismas, que en muchos casos le han llevado a ser un objeto de culto underground. Levine ha conseguido una clientela llena de celebridades entre las que destacan Lady Gaga, The Black Eyed Peas, Bruno Mars y los Scissor Sisters. Sin duda, esta es la línea comercial, inicialmente soñada por un niño de 10 años de edad, que se está convirtiendo en una estrella, no sólo debido a su clientela, sino por méritos propios.

Page 48:
Asher Levine

Page 49:
Autumn Winter 2011
Image courtesy of Asher Levine

On these pages:
Autumn Winter 2011
All images courtesy of Asher Levine

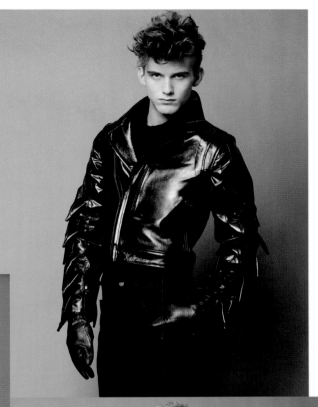

On these pages:
Spring Summer 2012
Photography: Kat+Duck

Asher Levine Disease #6

On these pages:
Spring Summer 2012
Photography: Kat+Duck
Illustration by Asher Levine

ALBERTO PURAS

www.albertopuras.com
MADRID
Spain

Alberto Puras was born in Madrid. Puras completed his studies in fashion design at the Instituto Europeo di Design, in the Spanish capital, and soon after he moved to New York to collaborate with the Russian designer Lika Volkova on her brand SANS. At that time, he tries to develop his own language in fashion and improving his technique. Back to Madrid, Puras decided to start his own label presenting his first menswear collection at the Ego during the Madrid Fashion Week. The collection was a success, and Puras received amazing reviews from the fashion critics. That same year he was selected to present the same collection in the Art'n BLOOM event in Brussels, and simultaneously receives the proposal to start selling his clothes in DO, a new concept store in Madrid. Alberto Puras is currently working hard on his second collection challenging himself by introducing his first garments for women.

Alberto Puras nació en Madrid. Puras finaliza sus estudios de diseño de moda en el Instituto Europeo di Design, en la capital española y poco después se traslada a Nueva York para colaborar con la diseñadora rusa Lika Volkova y su marca SANS. Por entonces, desarrolla su propio lenguaje en moda y mejora su técnica. De vuelta a España, se instala en un pequeño estudio de la calle Sagasta de Madrid. Es entonces cuando decide presentar su primera colección masculina en el Ego durante el Madrid Fashion Week. La colección recibe muy buenas críticas. Posteriormente es seleccionado para presentar su colección dentro del certamen Art'n BLOOM en Bruselas y también recibe la propuesta de empezar a vender sus prendas en DO, un nuevo *concept store* en Madrid. Actualmente Alberto Puras trabaja en su segunda colección con la que pretende retarse a sí mismo introduciendo prendas para mujer.

Page 56:
Alberto Puras

Page 57:
Collage
Spring Summer 2012
Photography: Ugo Cámera

On these pages:
Collage
Spring Summer 2012
Photography: Falkwyn de Goyeneche

On these pages:
Spring Summer 2012
Photography: Ugo Cámera
Illustrations by Alberto Puras

On these pages:
Spring Summer 2012
Photography: Ugo Cámera
Illustrations by Alberto Puras

GEORGE BEZHANISHVILI

www.georgebezhanishvili.com
NEW YORK CITY

George Bezhanishvili, as a label, was officially launched in 2008 when the first collection called *Long Haired Child* was presented in Vienna.
It was the menswear Autumn Winter 2008/2009 collection. Bezhanishvili is a Georgian born fashion designer, graduated from the University of Applied Arts in Vienna, Austria, under professors Veronique Branquinho and Bernhard Willhelm. With his first collection, he won the Swiss Textile Prize in 2008 along with the SONG Concept Store Award, continuing with *Jheronymus* collection in 2009 at the London Graduate Fashion week. That same year Bezhanishvili interned at the Fabrics Interseason while becoming the first prize winner of the Fondazione Claudio Buziol International Fashion Competition.

In 2010, *A Day Before Confession* collection was presented on a runway show at the Berlin Fashion week, and Bezhanishvili was selected to do the Camper Master Craft workshop in Mallorca, Spain. In 2011 he became the Rondo Voeslauer Fashion Award winner for his diploma work named *ODA*, and the Austria Ministry of Culture and Education award as an outstanding artist of the year for his effort in the fashion design throughout the past six years. From 2011 Bezhanishvili lives and works in New York City.

George Bezhanishvili, como marca, se inauguró oficialmente en el 2008, cuando la primera colección Long Haired Child fue presentada en Viena. Era la colección otoño invierno 2008/2009. Bezhanishvili nació en Georgia y se graduó en la University of Applied Arts de Viena, Austria, con los profesores Veronique Branquinho y Bernhard Willhelm. Con su primera colección, ganó el Swiss Textile Prize en el 2008 y el SONG Concept Store Award. Más tarde presentó en el 2009 en Londres su segunda colección, *Jheronymus*, en la London Graduate Fashion week. Ese mismo año Bezhanishvili entró en la Fabrics Interseason, ganando el primer premio de la Fondazione Claudio Buziol International Fashion Competition.

En el 2010, su colección *A Day Before Confession* se presentó en la pasarela de la semana de la moda de Berlín, y Bezhanishvili fue seleccionado para realizar el Camper Master Craft workshop en Mallorca, España. En el 2011 fue el ganador del Rondo Voeslauer Fashion Award por su colección *ODA*, y también el premio Austria Ministry of Culture and Education al artista destacado del año por su esfuerzo en el diseño de moda a lo largo de los últimos seis años. Desde 2011, Bezhanishvili, vive y trabaja en Nueva York.

Page 64:
George Bezhanishvili
by Peter Stanglmayr

Page 65:
Pants from *Oda*
Autumn Winter 2011-12
Top from *Jheronymus*
Autumn Winter 2010-11
Photography: Sidney Son
LeopardMilkshake Team

On these pages:
Oda
Autumn Winter 2011-12
Photography: Shoji Fujii
Illustrations by George Bezhanishvili

George Bezhanishvili

This page:
Oda
Autumn Winter 2011-12
Photography: Rosa Rendl

Left page:
Oda
Autumn Winter 2011-12
Photography: Sia Kermani
Illustrations by George Bezhanishvili

On the following pages:
A day before confession
Spring Summer 2011
Photography: Sia Kermani

SERHAT ISIK

www.serhat-isik.com
BERLIN
Germany

In-between classic and modernism, Serhat Isik creates a space where elegance and conceptual design collides. Isik was born in Germany in 1988. After graduating from the University of Applied Sciences Bielefeld in 2011, he moved to Berlin. Today Isik is working for Bless, a conceptual flagship store in Berlin, and concentrates on his master studies while running his label that bears his own name, Serhat Isik. Thrilled by the idea of man paying attention to little details, Serhat Isik aims a wardrobe imbued by masculinity and sensitivity.

Entre lo clásico y lo moderno, Serhat Isik crea un espacio donde colisionan la elegancia el diseño más conceptual. Isik nació en Alemania en 1988. Después de graduarse por la University of Applied Sciences Bielefeld en 2011, se trasladó a Berlín. Hoy en día, Isik trabaja para Bless, una tienda insignia conceptual en Berlín, y se concentra en terminar su master compaginándolo con la marca de ropa que lleva su propio nombre, Serhat Isik. Diseña para el hombre que presta atención a los pequeños detalles. Un armario repleto de masculinidad y sensibilidad.

Page73:
You don't have a brother and he like cheese
Autumn Winter 2012
Photography: Joscha Kirchknopf & Andrea Grambow

On these pages:
You don't have a brother and he like cheese
Autumn Winter 2012
Photography: Jennifer Endom
Illustration by Serhat Isik

On these pages:
You don't have a brother and he like cheese
Autumn Winter 2012
Photography: Jennifer Endom
Illustration by Serhat Isik

On these pages:
You don't have a brother and he like cheese
Autumn Winter 2012
Photography: Joscha Kirchknopf
& Andrea Grambow
Illustration by Serhat Isik

BLAAK

blaak.co.uk
LONDON
England

Sachiko Okada and Aaron Sharif started the brand in 1998, as an experimental collaboration whilst studying at Central Saint Martins in London. The aim of the collaboration was to develop a style that is new yet believable. It's a style that does not isolate but enhances the wearer. They called it BLAAK after the colour for its transformative quality that symbolically purifies and regenerates. By the time of their graduation in 1999, the collection was sold internationally to Browns, Liberty, Maria Luisa in Paris and Barneys New York, to name a few.

BLAAK still are at the forefront of fashion a decade on, staying true to their original vision. They have grown a strong fan base of fashion editors and journalists such as Nicola Formichetti, Katy England, Tim Blanks, Nancy Rohde, and Hywel Davies. BLAAK is worn by Jean Michel Jarre, Catherine Deneuve, Kate Moss, Lara Stone, and Erin Wasson. Currently presenting Menswear collection on Paris fashion week schedule, BLAAK RAINBOW range for younger market in collaboration with Asos in London, and a bag range in collaboration with Headporter in Tokyo. They also do womenswear for special projects and commissions.

Sachiko Okada y Aaron Sharif iniciaron la marca en 1998, a modo de colaboración experimental, mientras estudiaban en la Central Saint Martins de Londres. El objetivo fue desarrollar un estilo nuevo y creíble. Un estilo que no aísla, sino que ensalza al usuario. Se llamaron BLAAK por el color negro, por su calidad de transformación que, simbólicamente, se regenera y se purifica. Tras su graduación en 1999, la primera colección que diseñaron se vendió a a nivel internacional en Browns, Liberty, Maria Luisa en Paris y en Barneys New York.

Una década después, BLAAK, todavía están a la vanguardia de la moda, fieles a su visión original. Sus fans son editores de moda y periodistas como Nicola Formichetti, Katy England, Tim Blanks, Nancy Rohde y Hywel Davies. Celebridades como Jean Michel Jarre, Catherine Deneuve, Kate Moss, Lara Stone y Erin Wasson se visten de BLAAK. En la actualidad han presentado una nueva gama de ropa para los más jóvenes, BLAAK RAINBOW, en la semana de la moda de París en colaboración con Asos en Londres y una colección de bolsos en colaboración con Headporter en Tokio. Diseñan también ropa de mujer por encargo y para proyectos especiales.

Page 81:
Man Vs Machine
Autumn Winter 2009-10
Photography: Takay

On these pages:
Culture Clash
Spring Summer 2012
Photography: Takay

On the following pages:
Sketches assortment
Autumn Winter 2009-10
Spring Summer 2009
Autumn Winter 2010-11
All illustrations by BLAAK

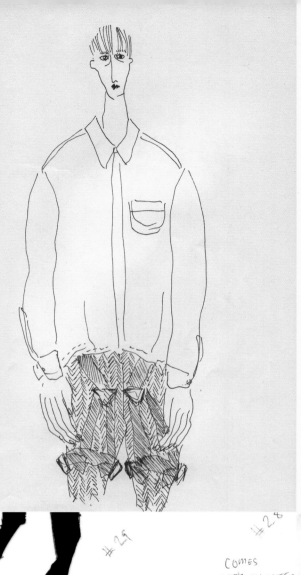

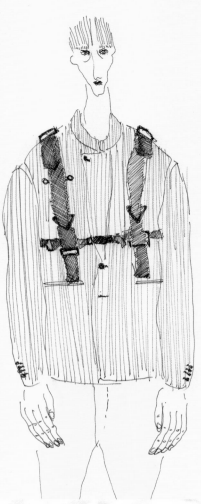

USING. — 45 BLOCK.

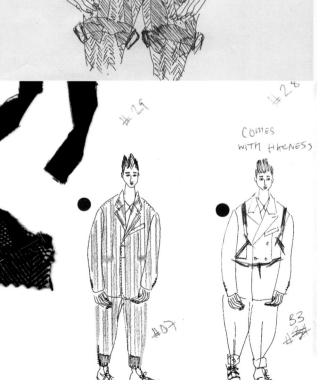

#29

#28

COMES
WITH HARNESS

#07

33

#23 PANTS. JK INSID STRAP.
○ WOOL / COTTON
STRIPE with 3M tape

○ BARATHEA
NAVY FELT

○ SCARATZ SILVE
○ BARATHEA
with 3.P

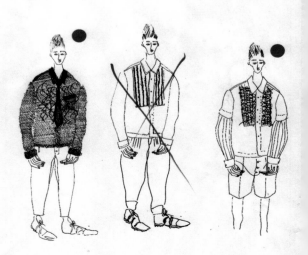

BLACK CREPE.

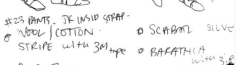

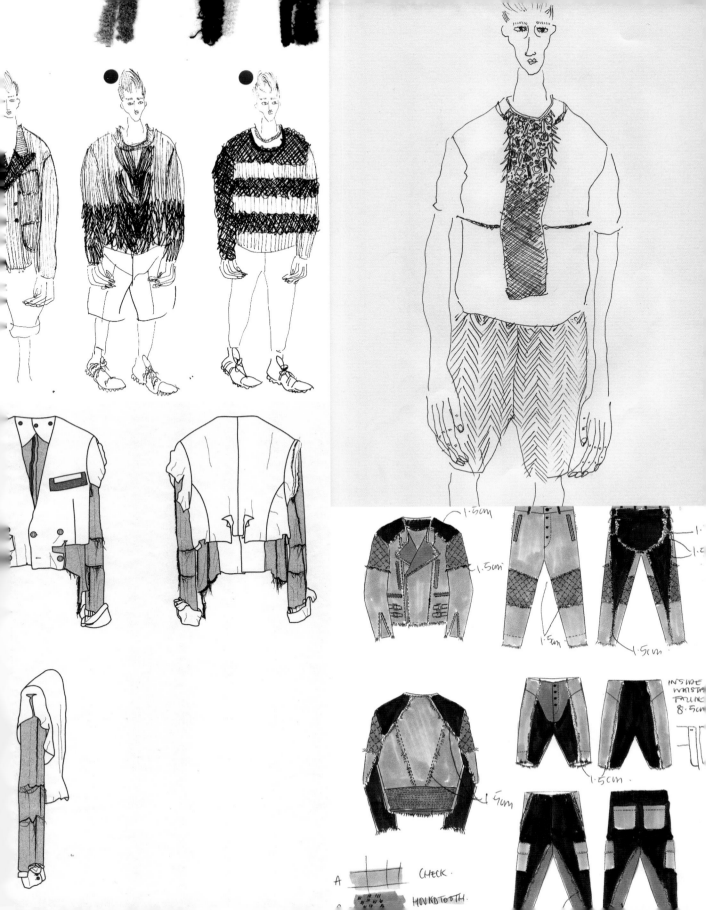

A   CHECK.

HOUNDTOOTH.

INSIDE
WAISTA
FALLING
8.5cm

1.5cm

This page:
Maximum or Minimum
Autumn Winter 2011-12
Photography: Takay
Illustration by BLAAK

Left page:
Buffalo Solider
Autumn Winter 2008-9
Gymnopédies
Spring Summer 2007
Photography: Takay

LUIS MANTEIGA

luismanteiga.com
BARCELONA
Spain

Luis Manteiga was born August 25, 1982, in Segovia, Spain. He began his career by studing fashion styling in the city of Granada, Spain, where he took classes in the Centro de Estudios Escénicos of Andalusia, where he learned the intricacies of theatrical costumes, and worked as a costume designer for several plays. After that Manteiga decided to complete his fashion studies in the Escuela Superior de Diseño y Moda Felicidad Duce in Barcelona, where he began to feel attracted by handbag and swimwear design. It was in Barcelona where he had the opportunity to do internships with fashion designers Gori de Palma and Manuel Albarran.

Shortly after that he created his own label and Manteiga won multiple awards, like the Mustang Fashion Weekend award 2009, best newcomer designer of Castilla León 2010, the Almacén de Ideas first prize at the Pasarela Abierta de Murcia 2010, or best designer at Modafad 2010, in Barcelona. Luis has presented his amazing collections in several showrooms such as the Ego de Cibeles in Madrid, and in the 080 in Barcelona. He have presented them in runways like the OFF, and the 080 during the Barcelona Fashion Week, and in the Ego Cibeles during the Madrid Fashion Week. Luis Manteiga is still deciphering the secrets behind his antagonistic collections.

Luis Manteiga nace en Segovia un 25 de agosto del 1982. Inicia su carrera en el mundo de la moda estudiando estilismo de indumentaria en la ciudad de Granada y en el Centro de Estudios Escénicos de Andalucía, donde aprende los entresijos del vestuario de teatro y trabaja como figurinista para obras de teatro. Poco después Manteiga decide completar sus conocimientos en la Escuela Superior de Diseño y Moda Felicidad Duce en Barcelona, donde empieza a sentirse atraído por el diseño de bolsos y las ropa de baño. En Barcelona tuvo la oportunidad de hacer prácticas con diseñadores como Gori de Palma o Manuel Albarran.

Nada más crear su propia marca, Manteiga comienza a ganar multitud de premio, como el Mustang Fashion Weekend 2009, el del mejor diseñador novel de Castilla León 2010, primer premio Almacén de Ideas en la Pasarela Abierta de Murcia 2010 o el del mejor diseñador del Modafad 2010 en Barcelona. Luis ha presentado sus colecciones en los showroom del Ego de Cibeles en Madrid y en el del 080 en Barcelona, y ha desfilado en el OFF de la Semana de la Moda de Barcelona, en la pasarela Ego Cibeles durante el Madrid Fashion Week y en la pasarela 080 Barcelona Fashion Week. Luis Manteiga continúa descifrando los secretos de sus colecciones antagónicas.

Page 90:
Luis Manteiga by
Francisco Ubeda Llorente

Page 91:
Cosmogonía
Photography: Biel Sol

On these pages:
Frontera Brekenstein
Autum Winter 2012-13
Photography: Ugo Camera
Illustration by Luis Manteiga

Luis Manteiga

On these pages:
Sayat Nova
Spring Summer 2012
Photography: Ugo Camera
Illustrations by Luis Manteiga

This page:
Cosmogonía
Photography: Alicia Calle

Left page:
Cosmogonía
Photography: Biel Sol
Illustrations by Luis Manteiga

Page 98:
Cosmogonía
Photography: Alicia Calle

Page 99:
Cosmogonía
Photography: Biel Sol

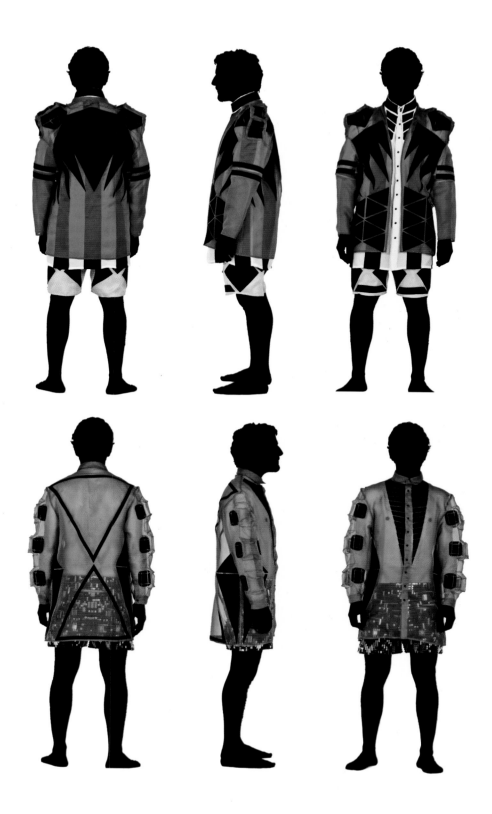

CONQUIS—
TADOR

www.conquistador.eu
LYON
France

German born, Athens based, Greek stylist, photographer, creative director and part time creative consultant, Tassos Sofroniou started his successful career from the age of 14, along with his academic studies in photography and history of fashion and graphic design. After a successful career mainly as a fashion stylist in Greece, Tassos relocated to London in 1995. He worked for three years as a P.A to his icon and fairy godmother of contemporary style, British stylist Isabella Blow. After a decade of productive and important collaborations with photographers Richard Avedon and David LaChapelle, and magazines such as *The Face, Surface, Interview*, British *GQ, Sunday Times Style, Exit*, and *Scene*, he returned to Greece to continue his styling career this time adding fashion photography and creative direction in his resume. In February 2010 the first ideas and sketches were drawn and soon after Conquistador was born.

The brand was launched in Athens in September 2010 during Vogue's Fashion's Night Out, at the historical hotel Grand Bretagne, with an installation mixing clothes, video, art and live original music composed on the spot, which received an encouraging and overwhelming response from press and buyers. Conquistador balances style and originality in equal measures. Mostly handmade and designed as luxurious as a man can be, the collections are shaping an exciting new brand that mostly inspired by the all American college hoodie but totally reshaped and deconstructed with contemporary historical references and multifunctional styling options.

Tassos Sofroniou, nacido en Alemania y con sede en Atenas, es estilista, fotógrafo, director y consultor creativo, comenzó su exitosa carrera con tan solo 14 años estudiando fotografía, historia de la moda y diseño gráfico. Después de trabajar como estilista de moda en Grecia, Tassos se instaló en londres en 1995 y trabajó durante tres años para su icono y hada madrina la estilista inglesa Isabella Blow. Tras una década de importantes colaboraciones con fotógrafos como Richard Avedon o David LaChapelle y con revistas como *The Face, Surface, Interview, GQ,* inglés, *Sunday Times Style, Exit*, y *Scene*, decide volver a Grecia para continuar con su carrera como estilista, pero esta vez incluyendo en su currículum sus primeros trabajos como fotógrafo de moda y director creativo. En febrero del 2010 sus primeros bocetos e ideas se materializaron en Conquistador, su propia marca de ropa.

La marca se lanzó al mercado en Atenas en septiembre del 2010 durante la Vogue's Fashion's Night Out, en el histórico hotel Grand Bretagne, con una instalación mezclando ropa, video, arte y música original en directo, recibiendo una alentadora y abrumadora respuesta por parte de críticos y compradores. Conquistador mezcla estilo y originalidad a partes iguales. La mayoría de las prendas, diseñadas para el hombre amante del lujo, están hechas a mano y sus colecciones se inspiran sobre todo en la típica sudadera universitaria americana con capucha, pero totalmente remodelada y deconstruída con referencias históricas contemporáneas y todas las opciones multifuncionales de su estilo.

Page 102:
Tassos Sofroniou
by Nikos Kousthenis

Page 103:
Salvation
Autumn Winter 2010
Photography: Tassos Sofroniou

On these pages:
Artesanal
Limited edition custom made
leather apparel
Autumn Winter 2012
Photography: Tassos Sofroniou

On the following pages:
Spring Summer 2012
Photography: Tassos Sofroniou

This page:
Autumn Winter 2012
Photography: Tassos Sofroniou

Right page:
Autumn Winter 2011
Photography: Tassos Sofroniou

ETXEBERRIA

www.etxeberria.com.es
BARCELONA
Spain

Roberto López Etxeberria was born in 1976 in Éibar, Spain. After studying fashion design at the Escuela Superior de Diseño y Moda Felicidad Duce in Barcelona, Roberto worked as an assistant for fashion designer Sergei Povaguin between 2005 and 2008; the same year he created his own brand, ETXEBERRIA, specializing in menswear.

Between 2008 and 2010, he attended to Pasarela Vigo, with his small collections *Night Calls* and *Dress Code*, and in Creamoda Bilbao with *Portraits*, receiving respectively an accésit, a second prize and a first prize. In 2011 he presented two complete collections on the Ego de Cibeles during the Madrid Fashion Week, *La piel que habito* Autumn Winter 2012, and *Jour de fête*, Spring Summer 2012, both winners of the L'Oréal award for best collection. After that, the brand was selected to represent Spain in the La Maison de la Création of Marseille second edition, and he was invited by the Spanish Embassy in Austria to introduce the collection *La piel que habito* in the Vienna Fashion Week, and exhibited the same collection in the Brooklyn Fashion Week in New York City, getting a great success on the international press. The brand recently presented *Winter Journey*, their Autumn Winter 2012-13 collection in the OFF Mercedes Benz Fashion Week in Madrid.

Roberto López Etxeberria nació en Éibar, Guipúzcoa, en 1976. Tras estudiar diseño de moda en la Escuela Superior de Diseño y Moda Felicidad Duce de Barcelona, Roberto trabajó como asistente del diseñador de moda Serguei Povaguin entre del 2005 al 2008, y ese mismo año crea su propia firma, ETXEBERRIA, especializada en moda masculina.

Entre 2008 y 2010, la firma concurrió con pequeñas colecciones en la Pasarela Vigo con las colecciones *Night Calls* y *Dress Code*, y en Creamoda Bilbao, con la colección *Portraits*, recibiendo respectivamente un accésit, el segundo premio y un primer premio. En 2011 presentó dos colecciones completas en la pasarela El Ego de Cibeles durante el Madrid Fashion Week, *La piel que habito*, otoño invierno 2012, y *Jour de fête* primavera verano 2012, ganando con ambas y de forma consecutiva el Premio L'Oréal a la mejor colección. Después de todos estos éxitos cosechados, la firma fue seleccionada para representar a España en la segunda edición de La Maison de la Création de Marseille, fuer invitada por la Embajada Española en Austria para presentar la colección *La piel que habito* en el Vienna Fashion Week, y desfiló en la Brooklyn Fashion Week de Nueva York, obteniendo un gran éxito y una importante repercusión en la prensa internacional.

Page 108:
Roberto López Etxeberria

Page 109:
Portraits
Autumn Winter 2010
Photography: Juancar Hernández

On these pages:
Jour de fête
Spring Summer 2012
Photography: Ugo Camera

On these pages:
La piel que habito
Autumn Winter 2011
Photography: Ugo Camera

On these pages:
La piel que habito
Autumn Winter 2011
Photography: Ugo Camera
Illustration by Etxeberria

This page:
La piel que habito
Autumn Winter 2011
Illustration by Etxeberria

Right page:
Portraits
Autumn Winter 2010
Illustration by Etxeberria

SINPATRON

www.sinpatron.com
BILBAO
Spain

Sinpatron is the label, Alberto, is the self-taught fashion designer behind it. Sinpatron is very well known for its experimentation with fabrics and materials, in which prevails craftsmanshipm with a limited edition of garments production. Alberto is the head designer of Sinpatron, and he presents his collections twice a year in so many different runways like the Ego de Cibeles in Madrid, Modorrra in Bilbao, Iqons in Barcelona, Pasarela abierta de Murcia, and Pasarela South in Cádiz, Spain. Sinpatron has received several awards, such as the best fashion designer in the Benicassim International Festival in 2006, best menswear collection in Creamoda in 2007, and he was selected in 2010 with other nine international fashion designers to take part in the Who's Next catwalk show in Paris.

Sinpatron has also made costumes for the opera *La Boheme* for the Comunidad de Madrid, also costumes for music videos, and pop bands such as Chico y Chica, Lkan, Pierre Pascual, for dance company Bad in Bilbao, and dancers like Roberto Martinez and Barbara Sanchez, creating textile scenery for the Museo de Reproducciones Bilbaíno, and for the independent music festival Bilboloop. Sinpatron also works making styling for advertising campaigns.

Sinpatron es una firma de moda que comenzó su andadura de manera autodidacta hace seis años. La marca se caracteriza por su experimentación con los materiales, en la que prevalece lo artesanal y la producción seriada de prendas. Hasta la fecha ha desarrollado su labor presentando dos colecciones anuales en diferentes pasarelas: como el Ego de Cibeles en Madrid, Modorrra en Bilbao, Iqons en Barcelona, Pasarela abierta de Murci y en la Pasarela South en Cádiz. Sinpatron ha ganado varios premios, como por ejemplo el del mejor diseñador en el Festival Internacional de Benicàssim en el 2006, a la mejor colección masculina en el Certamen de Creamoda en 2007 y seleccionado en 2010 junto con otros nueve diseñadores internacionales para participar y desfilar en el Who´s next en París.

Sinpatron ha realizado además el vestuario para la opera *La Boheme* para la comunidad de Madrid, vestuario para videoclips y grupos musicales como Chico y Chica, Lkan o Pierre Pascual, compañías de danza como el Bad en Bilbao y para bailarines como Roberto Martínez o Bárbara Sánchez, así como escenografías textiles para el Museo de Reproducciones Bilbaíno y el festival de música independiente Bilboloop y estilismos para campañas de publicidad.

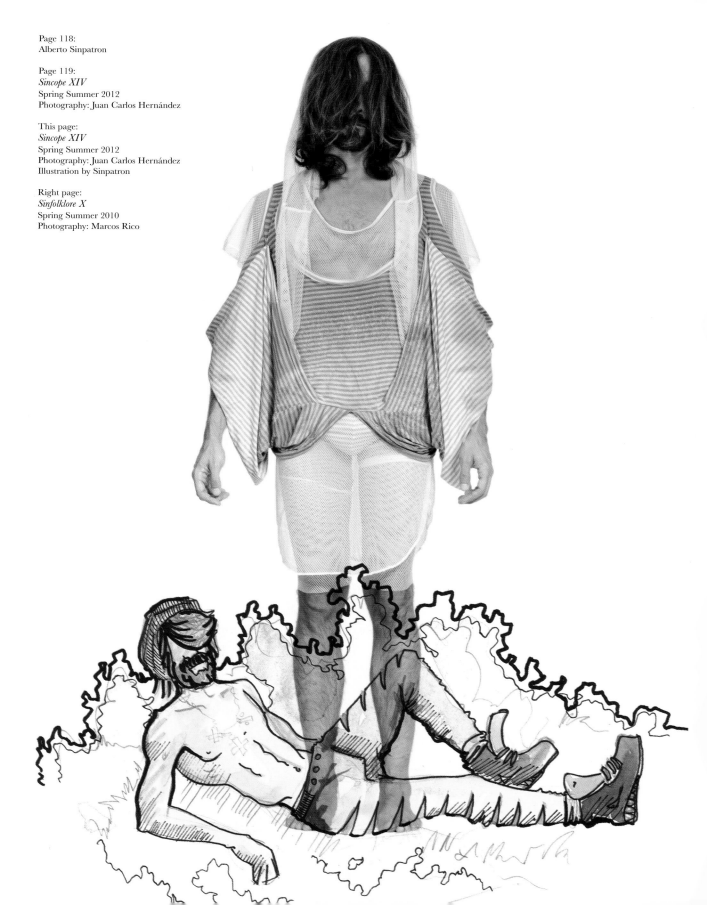

Page 118:
Alberto Sinpatron

Page 119:
Sincope XIV
Spring Summer 2012
Photography: Juan Carlos Hernández

This page:
Sincope XIV
Spring Summer 2012
Photography: Juan Carlos Hernández
Illustration by Sinpatron

Right page:
Sinfolklore X
Spring Summer 2010
Photography: Marcos Rico

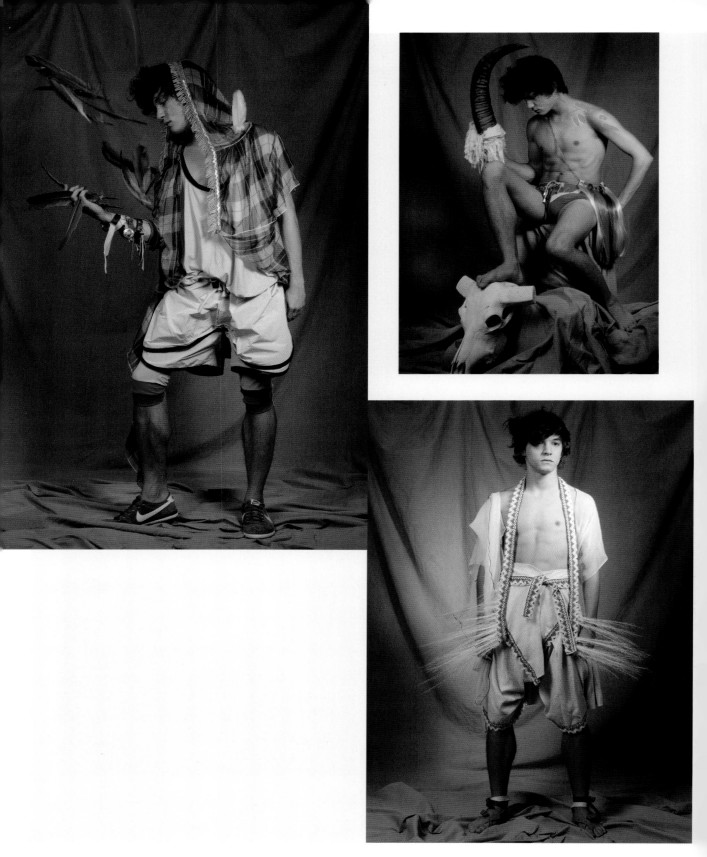

On these pages:
Todojuntoysinacento VIII
Spring Summer 2009
Photography: Pasarela Cibeles

HYAKINTH

www.hyakinth.com
POLAND

Hyakinth is the fast growing brand new label by young Polish designer Jacek Kłosiński. Born in 1985, Jacek is a graduate of Academy of Fine Arts in Lodz, Poland, where he studied both fashion design and textile print. When he started to design, Jaccek found that he was able to express ideas, stories, and moods more effectively through clothing than he ever managed to do through art. The challenge of having to overcome the restriction of menswear has motivated him to be a menswear designer. In contrast to womenswear, menswear is very much rooted in tradition, in which what is appropriate for a man to wear is clearly defined. Jacek's work is very much based on the tension created in the process of testing these limits. A good example is the jacket, a classic men's garment, Jacek's transforms it to a more fashion forward article of clothing, using his own digital printed fabrics.

Hyakinth es la marca propiedad del joven diseñador polaco Jacek Kłosiński. Nacido en 1985, Jacek se graduó en la Academy of Fine Arts en Lodz, Polonia, donde estudió diseño de moda e impresión textil. Cuando empezó a diseñar, Jacek se dio cuenta de que era capaz de expresar ideas, historias y estados de ánimo con más eficacia a través de la ropa de lo que nunca logró a través del arte. El desafío de tener que superar la restricciones en el diseño de ropa masculina le motivó a ser un diseñador de ropa de hombre. En contraste con la indumentaria femenina, la moda masculina está muy arraigada a la tradición, que limita obviamente la forma en la que debe vestirse un hombre libremente. Su trabajo se concentra mucho en romper estos límites. Un buen ejemplo es la chaqueta, una prenda de vestir típica masculina, a la que Jacek le da la vuelta al concepto usando tejidos impresos digitalmente.

Page 126:
Jacek Kłosiński

Page 127:
Autumn Winter 2011
Photography: Łukasz Brzeúkiewicz

On these pages:
Poland Fashion Week
Spring Summer 2012
Photography: Micha≥ TuliÒski

On these pages:
Spring Summer 2011
Photography: Łukasz Brzeúkiewicz

On these pages:
Spring Summer 2011
Photography: Łukasz Brzeúkiewicz

DANIEL PALILLO

danielpalillo.blogspot.com
HELSINKI
Finland

Daniel Palillo is a Helsinki based designer. Palillo's clothing is not relied to any ideologies it is the result of spontaneous actions and an open-minded attitude. The signature for his collections is a tragicomic sense of dark humour with oversized shapes. The collections are both for men and women. Actually Daniel Palillo's clothes are available worldwide in selected shops.

Inspired by the time he spent in America, Daniel Palillo's Spring Summer 2012 collection *Never Mind*, draws from the anarchy of the designer's teenage music heroes, while painting a portrait of his everyday lived experiences: Saturday evening soccer matches or Sunday morning cartoons. In a world of his own, Palillo has a penchant for the monstrous and the symbolic. Staying inside his brand aesthetic, where enormous proportions meet three-dimensional structures and morbid graphics, the new designs take the trademark patchworks and cut outs to another level, stretching in both shape and size. He never mind the introduction of basic colours, the black humour always remains.

Daniel Palillo es un diseñador con base en Helsinki. La ropa de Palillo no se basa en ninguna ideología, es el resultado de la espontaneidad y de una mente abierta. La clave para cada colección es una tragicomedia, un humor negro y prendas oversize. Las colecciones son tanto para hombres como para mujeres y se encuentran disponibles las tiendas más selectas a nivel internacional.

Su última colección *Never Mind* está inspirada en el tiempo que Daniel pasó en América, en la música que escuchaba en su adolescencia, mientras pintaba retratos de sus vivencias cotidianas: los partidos de fútbol de los sábados por la noche o los dibujos animados de los domingos por la mañana. Palillo siente predilección por lo monstruoso y lo simbólico. Prendas de vestir de enormes proporciones se mezclan con estructuras tridimensionales y mórbidos gráficos. Los nuevos diseños elevan los patchworks y cortes de la marca a un nivel superior y por mucho que se incluy algún color básico nuevo, lo único que importa sigue siendo siempre el humor negro.

This page:
Never Mind
Spring Summer 2012
Photography: Paavo Lehtonen

Opposite page:
Talking Heads
Autumn Winter 2011
Photography: Paavo Lehtonen
Illustration by Laura Laine

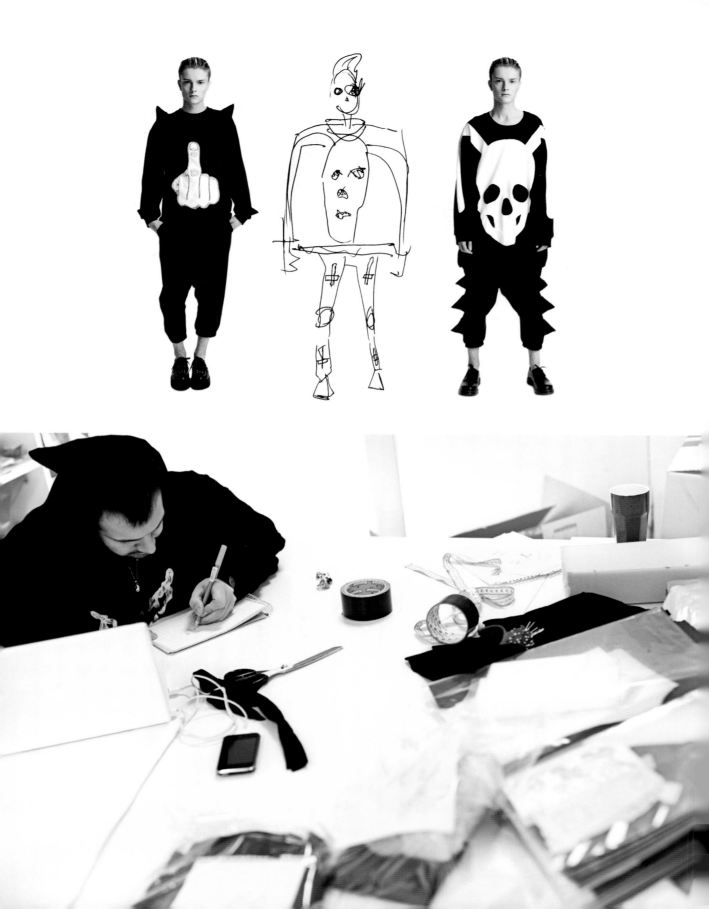

This page:
Never Mind
Spring Summer 2012
Photography: Paavo Lehtonen
Illustration by Daniel Palillo

Left page:
Never Mind
Spring Summer 2012
Daniel Palillo working at his studio
Photography: Paavo Lehtonen
Illustration by Daniel Palillo

LUKASZ STEPIEN

www.lukaszstepien.com
POLAND

Lukasz Stepien, fashion designer, brings to his brand his facets of artist and architect. He designs for men and women, but main challenge for him is menswear design. His projects underline masculinity and the power of fellow. The first success carried as stylist but very fast his creation was concerned by known clothing brands. The main stream of his activity is to design author collections which style balances on border of classic wear and avant-garde.

Lukasz Stepien loves to break conventions, but he creates garments that any man can wear. "Good dressed man, it is certain and creative" –says the designer. Lukasz Stepien takes inspiration from men's fashion history and from ordinary objects of the every day life. He loves to create unique projects, to memory falling. Lukasz connects always with his clients' needs, with his personal vision, but without forgetting how important is the comfort of wearing good sewing clothes. He is not a fashionista, he design pieces that doesn't break the rules of good tailoring.

Lukasz Stepien, diseñador de moda, aporta a su marca sus facetas de artista y arquitecto. Diseña para hombres y mujeres, pero el principal reto para él es la moda masculina. Trabajar como estilista de moda le hizo interesarse mucho por las marcas de ropa más conocidas. El *leit motiv* principal de su actividad es el diseño de sus colecciones de autor en las que se mezcla lo clásico y lo vanguardista.

A Lukasz Stepien le gusta romper con lo convencional pero diseña ropa que pueda ponerse cualquier hombre. "Un hombre bien vestido se siente seguro", afirma el diseñador. Para crear sus colecciones Lukasz se inspira en la historia de la vestimenta masculina y de cosas normales y corrientes del día a día. Crea piezas únicas pensando siempre en las necesidades de sus clientes, para no olvidar la importancia que tiene que las prendas estén confeccionadas con mucha calidad y que sean cómodas de llevar. A Lucasz le encanta romper con las reglas de la sastrería, huyendo siempre de lo ya establecido .

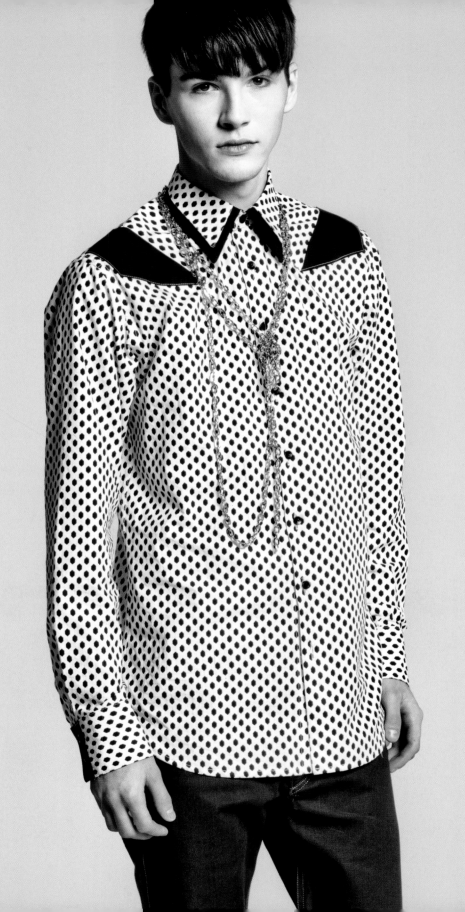

Page 144:
Łukasz Stępień by Furman

Page 145:
Autumn Winter 2011-12
Photography: Michal Kar
& Maciej Piorko

On these pages:
Autumn Winter 2011-12
Photography: Michal Kar
& Maciej Piorko
Illustration by Lukasz Stepien

This page:
Autumn Winter 2011-12
Photography: Michal Kar
& Maciej Piorko

Right page:
Boys Band
Autumn Winter 2011-12
Photography: Michał Kar
& Maciej Piórko

On the following pages:
Autumn Winter 2011-12
Photography: Michal Kar
& Maciej Piorko

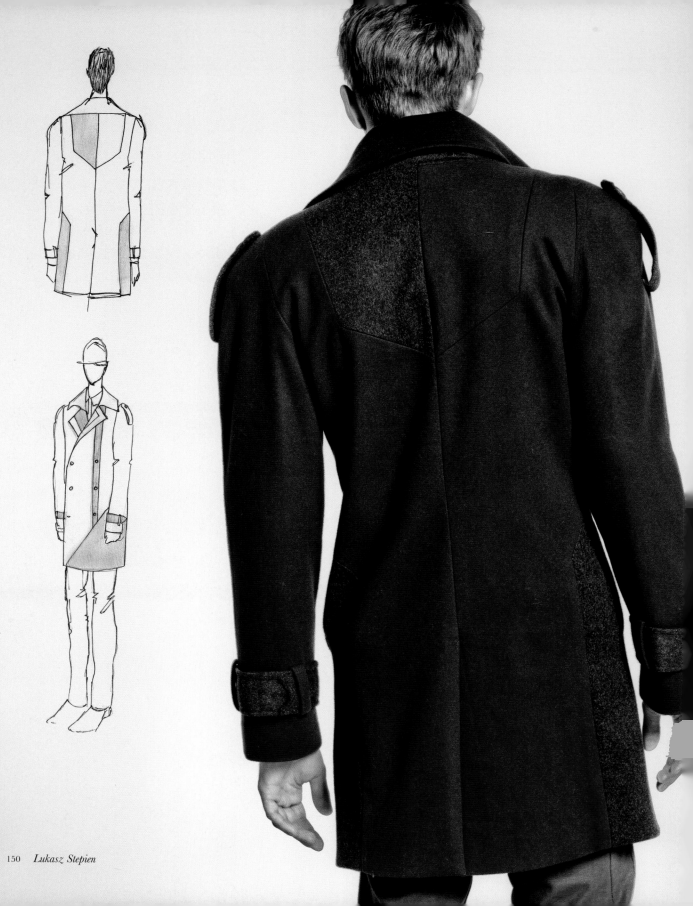

BRAIN& BEAST

www.brainandbeast.com
BARCELONA
Spain

In 1999, after finishing his studies of fine arts at the Universidad de Barcelona, Ángel Vilda, head designer of Brain & Beast, decided to study fashion design at the Universidad Politécnica de Madrid and at the London College of Fashion. Before establishing his own brand of clothing, he worked designing for a few mainstream brands.

Ángel has presented his collections at the CIRCUIT, the 080, and the Pasarela Gaudí in Barcelona, Cibeles and the SIMM in Madrid, and in the WORKSHOP and the RENDEZ-VOUS in Paris. Now, in Brain & Beast, he offers his point of view about what's a nowadays wardrobe for men and women. High quality and personality have always been his slogans, working for real people living in a real word. Ángel also continues teaching fashion design at the Institut Català de la Moda and costume design at the Instituto Europeo di Design, both of them in Barcelona, Spain. He has won several awards such as the Critics' Best Costume Designer Award and the Butaca Award for the best costume design in 2009.

En 1999, después de terminar su carrera de bellas artes en la Universidad de Barcelona, Ángel Vilda, fundador de Brain & Beast, decide estudiar diseño de moda en la Universidad Politécnica de Madrid y en el London College of Fashion en Londres. Antes de crear su propia marca, trabajó para algunas marcas de ropa muy conocidas.

Ángel ha presentado sus colecciones en el CIRCUIT, en el 080 y en la Pasarela Gaudí en Barcelona, en Cibeles y el SIMM en Madrid, y en el WORSHOP y el RENDEZ-VOUZ en París. Ahora, en Brain & Beast, ofrece su propio punto de vista sobre qué es lo que debería haber hoy en día en el armario ropero del hombre y la mujer. Calidad y personalidad han sido siempre sus eslóganes, trabajando para gente real que vive en un mundo real. Ángel también trabaja como profesor de diseño de moda en el Instituto Europeo di Design y en el Institut Català de la Moda, ambos en Barcelona. Ha ganado algunos premios como el Critics' Best Costume Designer Award y el Butaca Award al mejor diseñador de ropa en el año 2009.

Page 152:
Ángel Vilda by Noemí Jariod

Page 153:
Décalogue. Part I (Murk)
Autumn Winter 2011
Photography: Biel Sol

On these pages:
Décalogue . Part III (Magic)
Autumn Winter 2012-13
Photography: Ugo Camera

On these pages:
Décalogue. Part II (Rough)
Spring Summer 2012
Photography: Ugo Camera
Illustrations by Ángel Vilda

On these pages:
Décalogue. Part I (Murk)
Autumn Winter 2011
Photography: Biel Sol

On these pages:
Décalogue. Part I (Murk)
Autumn Winter 2012
Photography: Ugo Camera

ANDREA CAMMAROSANO

www.andreacammarosano.com
ANTWERP
Belgium

Andrea Cammarosano is an Italian-born, Antwerp-trained fashion designer. He studied fashion design and tailoring in Florence, Italy, and at the Royal Academy in Antwerp, Belgium, where he graduated in 2008. Upon graduation, Andrea received the MoMu Award, granted to a student. The resulting solo show at the MoMu Gallery in Antwerp was described as "an inimitable tribute to metamorphosis and the potential to create." The same year Andrea was selected as finalist in the ITS#7 Awards in Trieste, Italy. His graduation collection found place in the pages of *Dazed and Confused*, Russian *Vogue*, *Nylon Magazine*, *Mood*, and *Vogue Talent Italy*. After that Andrea worked for menswear designer Walter Van Beirendonck as an assistant, working on a footwear line and on the runaway collection. In that period Andrea also worked on a capsule line under his name, and was granted artistic residencies at the Museum Quartier, in Vienna, and The Arnhem Mode Biennale, in The Netherlands.

In 2010, Andrea established his own commercial label, under his name. This brand is informed by such different experiences as the avant-garde Belgian fashion and the free spirit of San Francisco, where Andrea lives and teaches; the collection is entirely manufactured in Italy, his country home, and sold in key stores in Paris, London and Antwerp.

Andrea Cammarosano estudió diseño de moda en Amberes, Bélgica y nació en Italia. Andrea estudió diseño de moda y sastrería en Florencia, Italia, y en la Royal Academy de Amberes, dónde se graduó en el 2008. Tras su graduación recibió el MoMu Award, que se concede a los estudiantes. Si primer show en solitario en el MoMu fue descrito como "un inimitable tributo a la metamorfosis y al poder de la creación". El mis año fue seleccionado como finalista en el concurso ITS#7 en Trieste, Italia. Su colección de graduación ha sido publicada en las páginas de Dazed and Confused, la edición rusa de la revista Vogue, Nylon Magazine, Mood, y en Vogue Talent Italy. Poco después Andrea trabaja como asistente para el diseñador Walter Van Beirendonck, creando una línea de zapatos y en las colecciones para los desfiles. En ese período Andrea trabajó en una línea de accesorios que estuvieron expuestas en el Museum Quartier, en Viena y en la Arnhem Mode Biennale, en los Países Bajos.

En el 2010, Andrea establece su propia firma comercial, bajo su propio nombre. La marca está influenciada por experiencias tan diferentes como la moda de vanguardia belga y el espíritu libre de la ciudad de San Francisco, donde Andrea vive y además trabaja como profesor. Las colecciones están totalmente fabricadas en Italia, su país natal, y se venden en tiendas claves en París, Londres y Amberes.

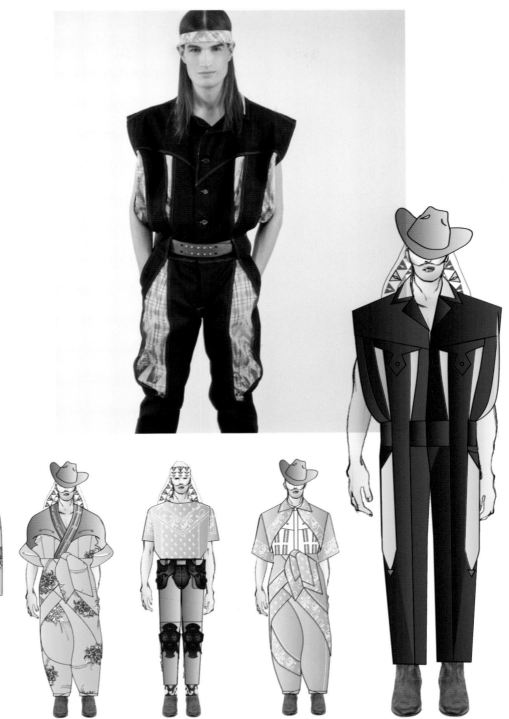

Page 162:
Andrea Cammarosano
Page 163:
East, West, Home Best
Spring Summer 2012
Photography: Deniz Buga

On these pages:
East, West, Home Best
Spring Summer 2012
Photography: Deniz Buga
Illustrations by Andrea
Cammarosano

On these pages:
East, West, Home Best
Spring Summer 2012
Photography: Deniz Buga

On these pages:
East, West, Home Best
Spring Summer 2012
Photography: Deniz Buga

KRIZIA ROBUSTELLA

www.kriziarobustella.com
BARCELONA
Spain

Krizia Robustella defines her brand style as *Sport Deluxe*. She loves to use sport garments of the last decades to create her own universe where comfort is merged in perfect harmony with luxury, shapes and fabrics that were until now something very informal.

Krizia Robustella is the brand for risky, eccentric and non-conformist people who feel the need to look different and to be observed during the day, without loosing the elegance and glamour that characterizes the nights in the big cities. People willing to express themselves individually through their outfit, mixing styles with no fear, following fashion in their own way.

Krizia Robustella define su estilo como *Sport Deluxe*. A Robustella le encanta usar prendas deportivas de las últimas décadas para crear su propio universo, donde el confort se combina en perfecta armonía con el lujo, las formas y tejidos que eran hasta ahora algo súper informal.

Krizia Robustella es la marca para gente excéntrica e inconformista que sienten la necesidad de tener un aspecto diferente y sentirse observados durante el día, sin perder la elegancia y el glamour que caracteriza a las noches en las grandes ciudades. Personas que quieren expresarse de forma individual a través de su atuendo, mezclando estilos sin miedo y siguiendo la moda a su manera.

Page 170:
Krizia Robustella by DizyDíaz

Page 171:
Quack Quack Boom Boom!
Autumn Winter 2012-13
Photography: Biel Sol

On these pages:
Quack Quack Boom Boom!
Autumn Winter 2012-13
Photography: Biel Sol

On these pages:
Lick my Ice Cream Baby
Spring Summer 2012
Photography: Ugo Camera
Illustration by Alma Esteban

On these pages:
Road Club Lovers
Autumn Winter 2011-12
Photography: Biel Sol
and DizyDíaz

This page:
Beautiful Beach
Spring Summer 2011
Photography: DizyDíaz

Left page:
Bang Bang Carajillo Gang
Autumn Winter 2010-11
Photography: Biel Sol

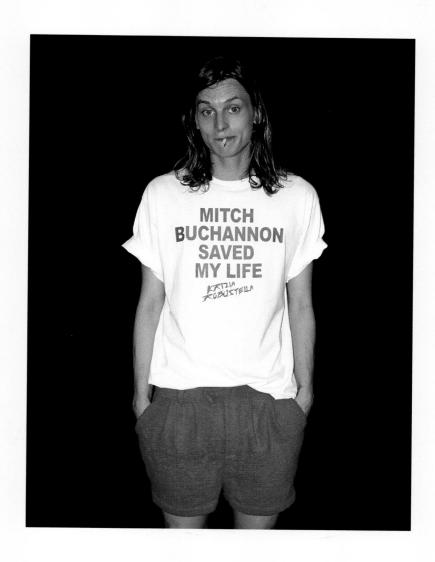

SIX LEE

www.sixlee.com
HONG KONG - ANTWERP

After graduating at The Royal Academy of Fine Arts Antwerp, Belgium, in 2009, Six Lee became the first Chinese who ever graduated in this Academy. Born in Hong Kong, Lee moved to London for a collaboration at the Alexander McQueen menswear team. The traditional British tailoring, translated into clean cuts and sharp lines, combined with soft colors and dreamy, boyish details result in unique silhouettes. As well as a new fresh level with modern twists and new proportions, to make an statement on traditional tailoring. As an overly romantic person, Lee gets inspired by the most diverse genres of music and films. The emotion he puts into writing poems or pressing flowers, will be found in every single piece from his hands. Carrying a touch of his love; never ever disappointing.

Después de graduarse en The Royal Academy of Fine Arts Antwerp, Bélgica, en 2009, Six Lee se convirtió en el primer chino graduado en esa academia. Nacido en Hong Kong, Lee se traslada a Londres para una colaboración con el equipo de moda masculina de Alexander McQueen. La sastrería tradicional inglesa, traducida en cortes limpios y afiladas líneas, combinada con colores suaves dan un resultado de ensueño con detalles juveniles y siluetas únicas. Su diseño es fresco y moderno, aportando proporciones nuevas a la sastrería más tradicional. Extremadamente romántico, Lee se inspira en los más diversos géneros de la música y el cine. La emoción que pone en escribir poemas o prensando flores, se traslada a cada una de las prendas que tocan sus manos, con un amor que nunca decepciona.

Page 180:
Six Lee by
Gabrielle Goyvaerts

Page 181:
We're all at the end
Autumn Winter 2012
Photography: Zeb Daemen

On these pages:
We're all at the end
Autumn Winter 2012
Photography: Zeb Daemen

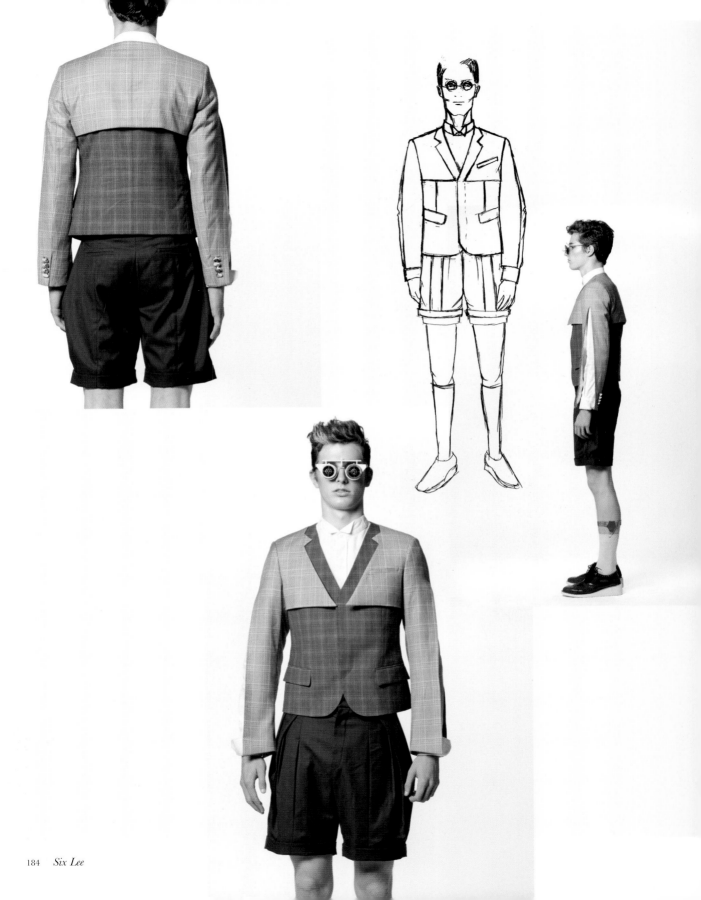

On these pages:
We're all in the dance
Spring Summer 2012
Photography: Koen Vernimmen
Illustration by Six Lee

On these pages:
We're all in the dance
Spring Summer 2012
Photography: Koen Vernimmen
Illustrations by Six Lee

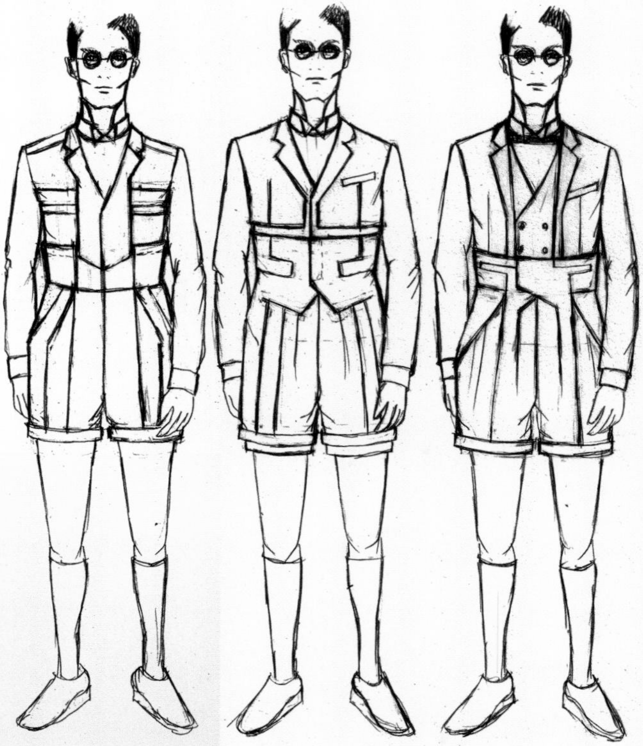

On these pages:
We're all in the dance
Spring/Summer 2012
Photography: Koen Vernimmen
Illustrations by Six Lee

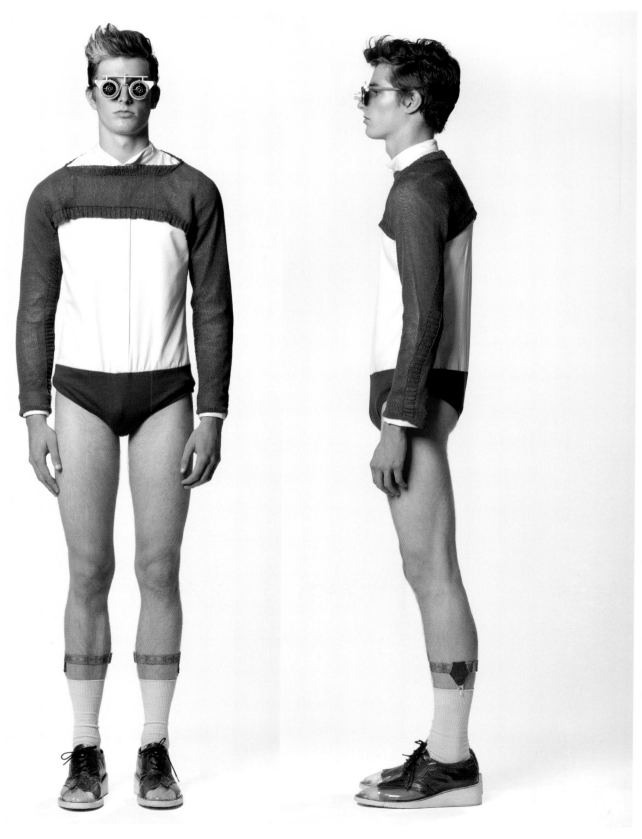

On these pages:
We're all in the dance
Spring/Summer 2012
Photography: Koen Vernimmen
Illustrations by Six Lee

MODAS CABEZÓN

modascabezon@gmail.com
MADRID
Spain

Juanma Jimenez launched his fashion brand Modas Cabezón in 2010, with the aim of covering the gap existing in men's shirts design. Juanma works as design assistant for the famous Spanish designer Carlos Diez Diez since 2000, in Madrid, Spain. He has worked as a costume designer for several films and plays, as well as a stylist for magazines like *Neo2, Calle 20* or *Vanidad,* and in advertising campaigns such as Lotería de Navidad, Coca-Cola, Playstation, *Marca,* Calvo, and for the Ministerio de Industria of Spain. During the weekends he loves to deejay on clubs, as a member of the Dj team "Gora ta Gora."

Modas Cabezón presents, twice a year, very exclusive and unique shirts just for men. Juanma loves to use mainly *vintage* fabrics on his creations, sometimes even older curtains. He says: "They have a quality and great prints, without complexes, which is very rare to find in the fabric industry these days."

Juanma Jiménez crea la marca Modas Cabezón en el año 2010, con el principal objetivo de cubrir el hueco existente en el diseño de camisería masculina. Juanma trabaja como asistente de diseño para el diseñador español Carlos Diez Diez desde el año 2000. Ha trabajado como figurinista en películas, como encargado de vestuario en obras de teatro, también como estilista para revistas como *Neo2, Calle 20* o *Vanidad* y en campañas de publicidad para Lotería de Navidad, Coca-Cola, Playstation, *Marca,* Calvo o el Ministerio de Industria español. Para desestresarse los fines de semana, a veces pincha en clubs como integrante del dúo de Djs "Gora ta Gora".

Modas Cabezón presenta cada seis meses sus colecciones de camisas para hombre. El uso de tejidos *vintage* predomina en la firma ya que, según él mismo dice: "Tienen unas calidades y unos estampados, sin complejos, que son difíciles de encontrar en los que se fabrican actualmente"

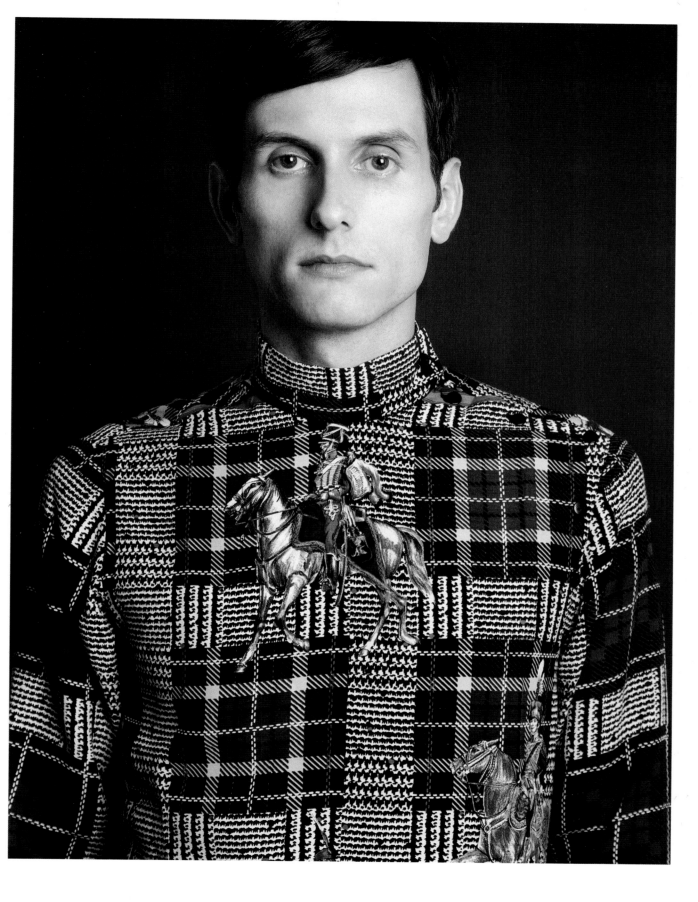

INV. 2011/12

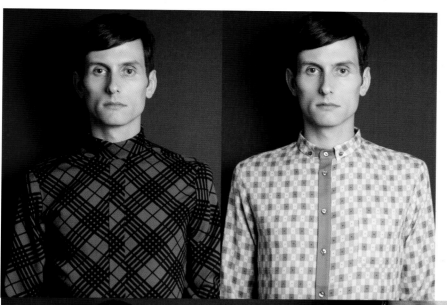

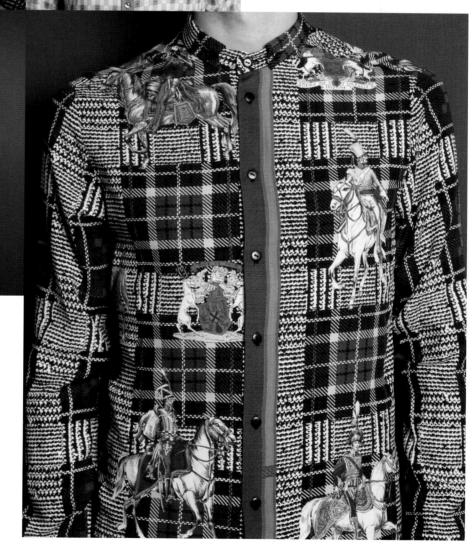

Page 192:
Juanma Jiménez by
César Segarra

Page 193:
Autumn Winter 2011-12
Photography: Pelagio Armenta

This page:
Autumn Winter 2011-12
Photography: Pelagio Armenta

Left page:
Photography: David Portela
Sketches by Juanma Jiménez

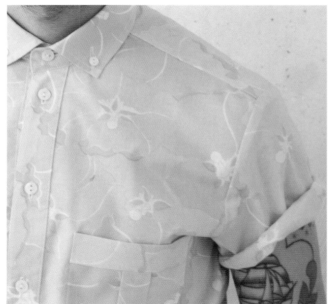

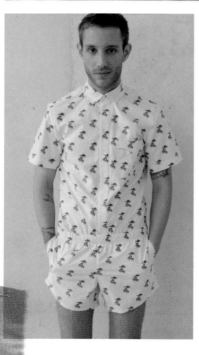

On these pages:
Autumn Winter 2010-11
Photography: Juanma Jiménez

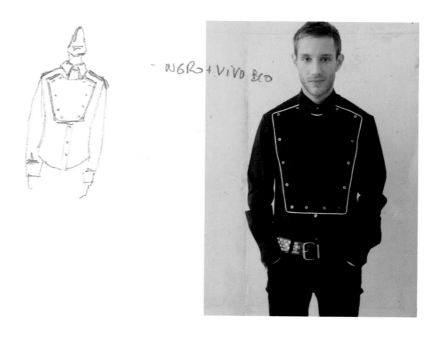

On these pages:
Autumn Winter 2010-11
Photography: Juanma Jiménez
Sketches by Juanma Jiménez

VISHL

www.vishland.com.br
BRASIL

The creative syncrony between Andreia Passos e Luiz Wachelke was responsible for the idea to create Vish!, back in 2007 in Brazil's southern city of Florianopolis. Shared interests, tastes and a similar lifestyle, which they name "creative life-style", led the duo to bring their complementary backgrounds and repertoirs together and face a clear challenge: transform their ideas and desires into clothes that reflect the freshness they look for in life. Despite the fact that they are both obsessed with fashion, neither has studied fashion per se: Luiz is a graphic designer and Andreia is a journalist. Their unique backgrounds bring particular creative processes and different takes on fashion to the brand.

With their minds attentive to behaviour trends, the designers explore their personal references and desires to create uncomplicated and fresh pieces. The need to be somehow connected to their creations make what seems to be unpretencious work, into something extremely rich and filled with personal references –which also reflects on the "do it yourself" spirit of this duo's work. The prints are result of detailed hand-drawn illustration and the pieces are always produced in limited numbers, so as to guarantee the exclusivity of their work.

La sincronización creativa entre Andreia Passos y Luiz Wachelke, fue la responsable de la idea de crear la marca Vish! Todo empezó en la ciudad de Florianopolis, al sur de Brasil. Compartían los mismos intereses, gustos y llevaban el mismo estilo de vida, que ellos mismos denominan: "creative life-style." Juntos decidieron convertir sus ideas y deseos en una marca de ropa que reflejara su manera de sentir la vida. Aunque ambos estén obsesionados por ese mundo, ninguno de los dos ha estudiado diseño de moda. Luiz es diseñador gráfico y Andreia es periodista, por lo que cada uno aporta a la marca su particular visión de la moda a nivel creativo.

Con sus mentes atentas a las tendencias, Vish! exploran sus referencias y deseos personales para crear prendas frescas sin complicaciones. La necesidad de estar conectados a todas y cada una de sus creaciones hace que en lugar de ser un trabajo sin pretensiones, sea algo extremadamente importante y lleno de referencias muy íntimas, lo cual se refleja en el espíritu "hazlo tú mismo" de este tándem de diseñadores. Los estampados son el resultado de ilustraciones, muy detallistas, dibujadas a mano. La producción de prendas es muy limitada, lo cual garantiza la exclusividad de su trabajo.

Page 200:
Andreia Passos and Luiz Wachelke
by Hugo Toni

Page 201:
Spring Summer 2012
Photography: Hugo Toni

This page:
Spring Summer 2012
Photography: Hugo Toni
Illustration by Vish!

Left page:
Spring Summer 2012
Exclusive print by Vish!

On these pages:
Spring Summer 2012
Photography: Hugo Toni
Illustration by Vish!

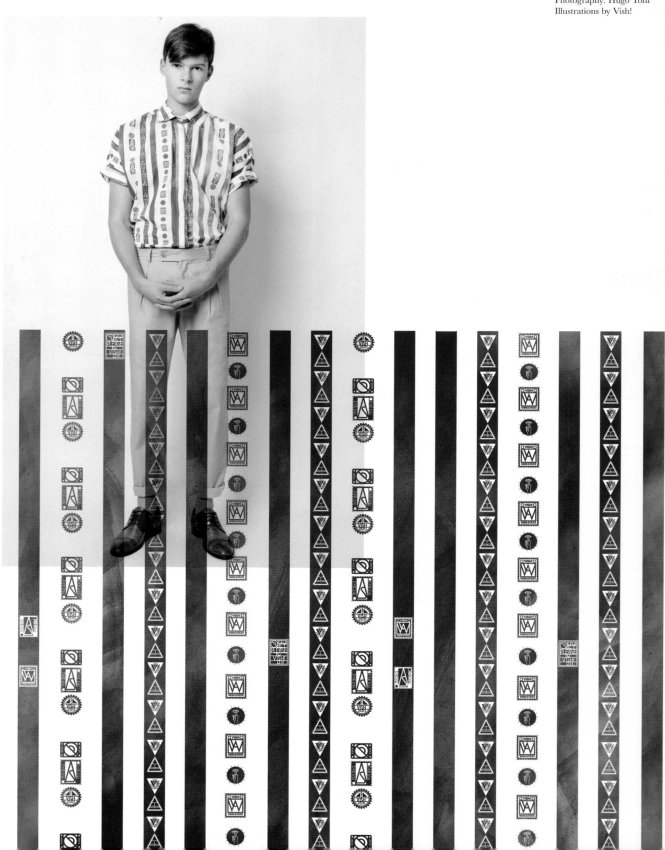

MANUEL BOLAÑO

www.manuelbolano.com
BARCELONA
Spain

Manuel Bolaño was born in Barcelona but grew up in Galicia. Bolaño moved back to Barcelona in 2002 where he studied fashion design at the Escuela Superior de Diseño y Moda Felicidad Duce. After working as part of Mango's design team, he decided to start working on his own first collection. In 2007 he won the Barcelona's Bread & Butter prize for the best collection; Murcia's open catwalk award, Madrid's young creators contest; Festival Noovo of Santiago de Compostela, and selected to take part in the Projecte Bressol, a fashion project launched by the Generalitat de Catalunya.

His first collection *Viudas* was shown in at the Barcelona 080's catwalk on September 2008. In March 2009, his collection *Peliqueiros* was presented as well at the 080 catwalk and it also was exhibited al the Rendez Vous Femme in Paris. His following collections *Canela en Rama* and *¿Por qué todo ha de ser de color de rosa?* were also a big success at the 080 catwalk. Manuel keeps presenting his collections twice a year, remaining in the top ranking as one of the best new Spanish fashion designers.

Manuel Bolaño nació en Barcelona, pero se crió en Galicia. En 2002 se traslada a Barcelona, dónde estudia diseño de moda en la Escuela Superior de Diseño y Moda Felicidad Duce. Después de trabajar durante un tiempo en el equipo de diseño de Mango, Bolaño decide iniciar su propia marca y crea su primera colección. En 2007 gana el premio de su promoción a la mejor colección en el Brad & Butter de Barcelona. Participa en la Pasarela Abierta de Murcia y gana premios en el concurso Jóvenes Creadores de Madrid, en el Festival Noovo de Santiago de Compostela y es seleccionado para participar en el Projecte Bressol de la Generalitat de Catalunya.

En Septiembre de 2008 presenta su primera colección *Viudas* en la pasarela del 080 de Barcelona. Después de su existoso debut le siguen vertiginosamente las colecciones *Peliqueiros*, presentada en la pasarela del 080 y en el Rendez Vouz Femme de Paris, y *Canela en Rama, ¿Por qué todo ha de ser color de rosa?* en el 080 también. Manuel sigue presentando sus colecciones dos veces al año, manteniéndose como una de las nuevas promesas del diseño de moda español.

Page 208:
Manuel Bolaño by Jordi Bartalot

Page 209:
¿Cómo reparar un corazón roto?
Spring Summer 2012
Photography: Pelagio Armenta

On these pages:
Un millón de promesas, un millón de cicatrices
Autumn Winter 2012-13
Images courtesy of Manuel Bolaño

On these pages:
¿Cómo reparar un corazón roto?
Spring Summer 2012
Images courtesy of Manuel Bolaño

On these pages:
¿Cómo reparar un corazón roto?
Spring Summer 2012
Photography: Pelagio Armenta

RAUN LAROSE

www.raunlarose.com
NEW YORK CITY

Raun LaRose was born in Brooklyn, and attended the Art Institute of New York where he majored in womenswear, graduating in 2009. Shortly after, he enlisted in the Fashion Institute of Technology for menswear design and tailoring. While in school, LaRose received an internship at *Vibe Magazine*, working in the fashion department. He learned how everything worked from an editorial standpoint; from how editors would pull looks for shoots to how they would create trend boards for stories to publish in the magazine. Later, he went on to intern for Zac Posen in Paris.

LaRose founded his company in 2009 as an independent designer and handles everything on his own. For now, his main focus is menswear. LaRose offers outerwear, blazers, shirting, and pants, but hopes to venture out into accessories in the future. Personally, LaRose loves the outdoors and is fascinated with technology. He loves haute couture, and if he could have any other job in the world, he would love to work as a couturier in a licensed house. LaRose loves the dedication and the time that goes into the garments, not to mention how beautiful the pieces are. In addiction Raun was named as the future in the category of menswear in the September issue of *Vogue Italia*.

Raun LaRose nació en Brooklyn, y estudió en el Art Institute of New York, donde se graduó en moda para mujer en el 2009. Poco después, se inscribió en el Fashion Institute of Technology en moda masculina y sastrería. Mientras estudiaba, LaRose hizo prácticas en *Vibe Magazine*, trabajando en el departamento de moda. Allí aprendió todo acerca del mundo editorial, desde como los editores organizan las sesiones de fotos, hasta como crean paneles de tendencias para crear los contenidos de una revista. Más tarde se trasladó a París para trabajar con Zac Posen.

LaRose fundó su propia compañía independiente en el año 2009. Desde entonces y en estos momentos su principal interés se centra la moda masculina. La firma abarca todo tipo de prendas exteriores, aunque LaRose no descarta crear también una línea de accesorios en el futuro. Personalmente, LaRose, está fascinado por las nuevas tecnologías y al mismo tiempo le encantaría trabajar al frente de alguna casa de alta costura importante europea. LaRose invierte todo su tiempo y dedicación en cada una de sus prendas que realiza. La revista *Vogue Italia* le mencionó en su número de septiembre como el futuro de la moda masculina.

Page 216:
Raun Larose

Page 217:
Autum Winter 2012
Photography: Casey Brooks

On these pages:
Autum Winter 2012
Photography: Casey Brooks

On these pages:
Forever Young
Spring Summer 2012
Photography: Nicolas Padron
Illustrations by Erin Dennison

On the following pages:
Forever Young
Spring Summer 2012
Photography: Nicolas Padron

SN.DJ

www.sndj.no
OSLO
Norway

Sahzene Nilhan Durmusoglu Johansen is the Oslo based menswear designer behind the brand Sn.DJ. She studied menswear at the Oslo National Academy of the Arts and in Central Saint Martins College of Art and Design, London. Upon graduating in Oslo, she was immediately favoured in *Vogue Italia*, and in August 2011, se won an award for the collection *More Weird Hits, More Weird Fits!* during the Oslo Fashion Week at the Cocoon New Talents Project. As a former music magazine editor, she always takes her starting point in music and blends it with other sources of inspiration such as street wear, gangs, found objects, experiments with fabric textures or simply her childhood memories from Istanbul. For every project, she starts with creating a soundtrack that refers to her inspirations. That's also why she always ends up with music related titles for her collections.

In her latest collection *More Weird Hits, More Weird Fits*, she blends lyrics and beats from South African techno artist Spoek Mathambo. The inspiration is the African masquerade costumes, photographer Phyllis Galembo's work, and the texture of a woven badge. Her process is a humoristic quest into certain concepts like camouflage, labelling and branding, consumerism, masquerade costumes and facemasks. She uses crochet and needle felting techniques, giant knits and digital prints as the signature style to her up-tempo menswear collection. The showpiece is an haute-couture bank robbery outfit covered in white crochet from top to toe.

Sahzene Nilhan Durmusoglu Johansen es la diseñadora, con sede en Oslo, detrás de la marca para hombre Sn.DJ. Estudió en la National Academy of the Arts en Oslo, y en la Central Saint Martins College of Art and Design de Londres. Tras su graduación en Oslo, sus primeros diseños aparecieron en el *Vogue Italia*, y en agosto del 2011, ganó un premio por su colección *More Weird Hits, More Weird Fits!* durante la semana de la moda de Oslo en el Cocoon New Talents Project. Como editora de revistas de música, siempre toma como punto de partida la música para crear sus colecciones, inspirándose en la moda urbana, las bandas callejeras, objetos que se encuentra o simplemente en los recuerdos de su infancia en Estambul. Cada proyecto comienza con la creación de una banda sonora, y esa es la razón por la que todos los nombres de sus colecciones están relacionados con la música.

En su última colección *More Weird Hits, More Weird Fits*, se inspira en las letras y sonidos del artista de música tecno sudafricano Spoek Mathambo, en los trajes de disfraces africanos y en el trabajo de fotógrafo Phyllis Galembo. El proceso es una búsqueda humorística de conceptos, como el camuflaje, el consumismo, los disfraces y las máscaras. Usa magistralmente las técnica del ganchillo dando forma a prendas tejidas de puntada gigante, junto con estampados digitales que definen el estilo de la marca. La pieza maestra es un traje de alta costura para "atracar bancos", hecho de ganchillo blanco que cubre desde la cabeza a los pies.

This page:
More Weird Hits, More Weird Fits
Photography: Daniel Tengs

Left page:
Personal sketchbook
Illustrations by SnDj

VICTOR VON SCHWARZ

www.victorvonschwarz.com
BARCELONA
Spain

Victor von Swcharz, a young fashion designer with Russian roots living in Barcelona, graduated in 2009. After his graduation Victor studied a degree in tailoring. After working for fashion designers Manuel Bolaño, Josep Font and Bibian Blue, Victor decided to create the independent brand that bears his own name.

Rockola, his first collection, was inspired by rock music and the 80s, and with *Abisalia*, his second collection, he tries to take us to the ocean floor through reinventions of basic rock style clothing. Silks, furs and wools decorated with studs and crystals, Victor von Swcharz lead us to the abyssal deserts.

Victor von Swcharz de origen ruso y afincado en Barcelona acabó sus estudios de diseño de moda en el año 2009, cursando después un master en sastrería. Tras un periodo de trabajo en los equipos de diseño de Manuel Bolaño, Josep Font y Bibian Blue, Victor decide crear la firma independiente que lleva su propio nombre.

La primera colección *Rockola*, estaba inspirada en la música rock y en los años ochenta y en *Abisalia*, su segunda colección, intenta transportarnos a los fondos oceánicos a través de reinvenciones de prendas básicas de estilo rockero. Sedas, pieles y lanas decoradas con tachuelas y cristales, nos llevan a los desiertos abisales.

Page 232:
Victor von Swcharz

Page 233:
Abisalia
Photography: Albert Madaula

This page:
Abisalia
Photography: Anne Galan

Right page:
Abisalia
Photography: Marta Soler
Illustrations by Victor von Swcharz

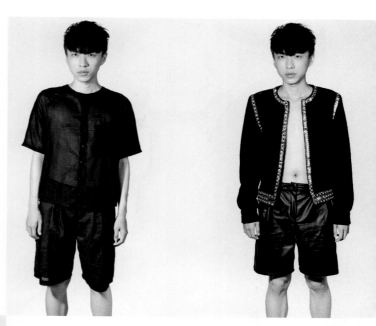

On these pages:
Rockola
Photography: Albert Madaula

TOM REBL

www.tomrebl.com
MILAN
Italy

Although Tom Rebl's collections are impeccably cut and created with love and care, clothes are not at the core of his universe. More important are attitudes, moods and statements. That's why music, art, performance, images and words have an important role in the whole package. Together with the clothes, those elements sum up, or rather clarify the kind of world Tom Rebl wants to project. In an attempt to examine today's male psyche; and at the same time his own, he takes his inspiration from the rebellion of past and present and blends this with notions of traditions and roots. The most important message Tom wants to communicate is pride in individuality. No wonder then he has often voiced his concern about the rigid and dictatorial stance of the mainstream fashion system in the past. His clothes are both inspired by and designed for confident outsiders.

Born and raised in Germany, educated at the notorious Central Saint Martins College of Art and Design,in London. Tom decided to establish his brand headquarters in 2008 in Italy, which is synonymous with outstanding quality, traditional tailoring and excellent craftsmanship. The mixture of superb technical skills and Tom's captivating creativity give his collections this extraordinary twist. The period in London before relocating to Italy were very influential in defining Tom's significant style and international appeal. Tom Rebl is known for his edginess, which is loved by rock stars and people who like to cultivate an avant-garde reputation.

Aunque las colecciones de Tom Rebl están impecablemente cortadas y creadas con mucho cariño y cuidado, la ropa no es el centro de su universo. Para Tom son más importantes las actitudes, los estados de ánimo y los principios. Es por esto que la música, el arte, las imágenes y las palabras tienen un papel muy importante en su filosofía de marca. Junto a la ropa, esos elementos se suman al mundo que Tom Rebl quiere proyectar. El mensaje más importante que Tom quiere difundir es el orgullo de la individualidad. No es de extrañar que a menudo ha expresado su preocupación por la postura rígida y dictatorial del sistema de la moda dominante en tiempos pasados. Su ropa está inspirada y diseñada al mismo tiempo para hombres seguros de sí mismos.

Nació y creció en Alemania y estudió en la conocida Central Saint Martins College of Art and Design de Londres. Tom decidió establecer el cuartel general de su marca en Italia, en el 2008, país que es sinónimo de calidad, sastrería tradicional y un artesanía excelente. La mezcla de sus excelentes habilidades técnicas y una cautivante mente creativa consiguen que Tom impregne sus colecciones de este giro extraordinario. Londres fue totalmente decisivo para la definición del estilo de Tom Rebl, una marca conocida por su estilo extremado de la cual se han enamorado estrellas del rock y personas a quienes les gusta cultivar una reputación de vanguardista.

Page 238:
Tom Rebl

Page 239:
Stargate 12
Autumn Winter 2012-13
Photography: Piero Visconti

On these pages:
Stargate 12
Autumn Winter 2012-13
Photography: Piero Visconti

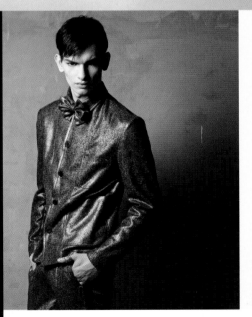

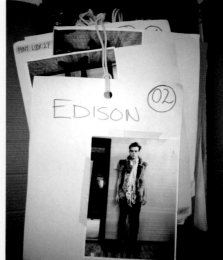

This page:
Tom Rebl's backstage
Photography: Marco Sfreddo

Right page:
Shocking Radiance
Spring Summer 2012
Photography: Tobias Scheuerer

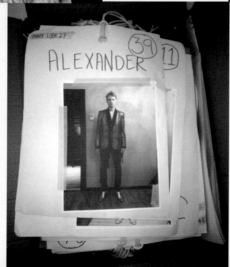

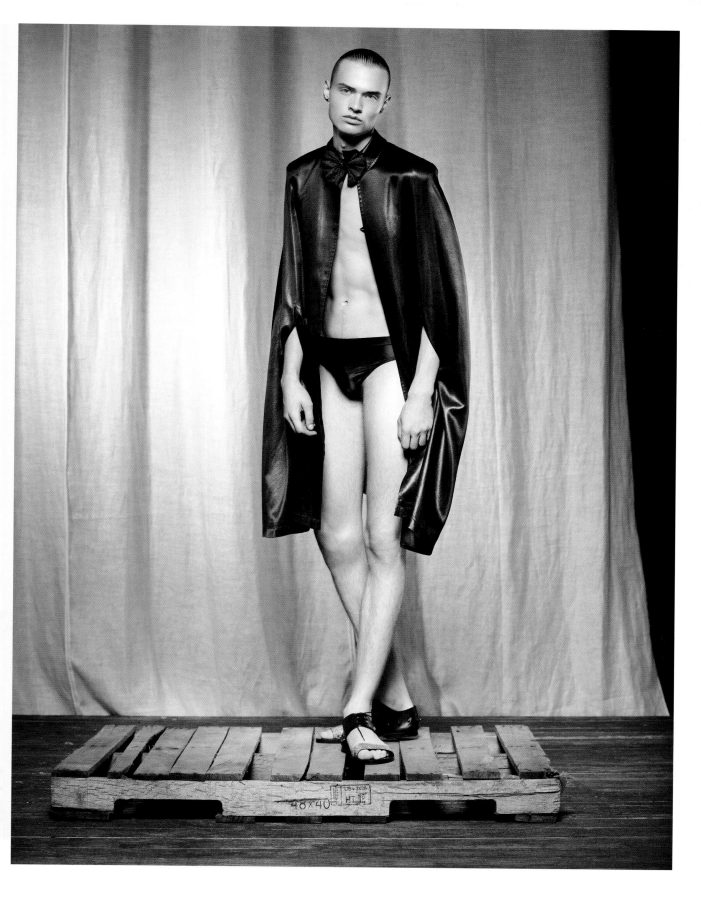

On these pages:
Shocking Radiance
Spring Summer 2012
Photography: Tobias Scheuerer

ASTRID ANDERSEN

www.astridandersen.com
LONDON - COPENHAGEN

Danish born Astrid Andersen graduated at the top of her class from the prestigious Royal College of Art in 2010. Her graduate collection received huge acclaim from the industry and jump-started the Astrid Andersen own label. It has been growing ever since as a result of fantastic press coverage riding high on the current trend for luxurious street style design. In 2010 Astrid Andersen was a finalist in IT'S#9 as well as being nominated as Talent 2010 by Vogue Italia. Whilst studying at the Royal College of Art Astrid also won the Brioni Creativity and Innovation Award and the River Island Student Bursary Award designing three looks for the high street retailer.

In 2011 Astrid held her first independent show in Copenhagen receiving enthusiastic appraisal and continuing to attract incredible international press and buyers, and she was also represented in London as a part of the widely acclaimed Fashion East installation in Somerset House. As a result Astrid Andersen is now based in both London and Copenhagen, using the best of two worlds by working and manufacturing from her studio in Copenhagen– reassuring the high level of quality of each garment whilst having the collections represented in the United Kingdom to ensure the creative philosophy behind the designs.

Danesa de nacimiento, Astrid Andersen se graduó como primera de su clase en la prestigiosa Royal College of Art, en el 2010. Su colección de graduación fue todo un éxito y recibió muy buenas críticas de la industria, lo cual alentó a Astrid para fundar su propia marca, la cual ha crecido mucho desde entonces gracias a la repercusión que ha ido teniendo en la prensa. En el 2010 Astrid fue finalista en el IT'S#9, y también fue nominada para el Talent 2010 por la prestigiosa revista Vogue Italia. Mientras estudiaba en el Royal College of Art Astrid también ganó el Brioni Creativity and Innovation Award y el River Island Student Bursary Award .

En el 2011 Astrid realizó su primer desfile independiente en Copenhague la cual fue acogida con mucho entusiasmo por la prensa internacional y los compradores, y también estuvo representada en Londres como parte de la aclamada Fashion East installation en Somerset House. Astrid Andersen vive y trabaja entre Londres y Copenhague, utilizando lo mejor de cada ciudad: trabaja y fabrica en su estudio en Copenhague, asegurándose un alto nivel de calidad en cada prenda, y presenta sus colecciones en Inglaterra para afianzar la filosofía creativa que hay detrás de sus diseños.

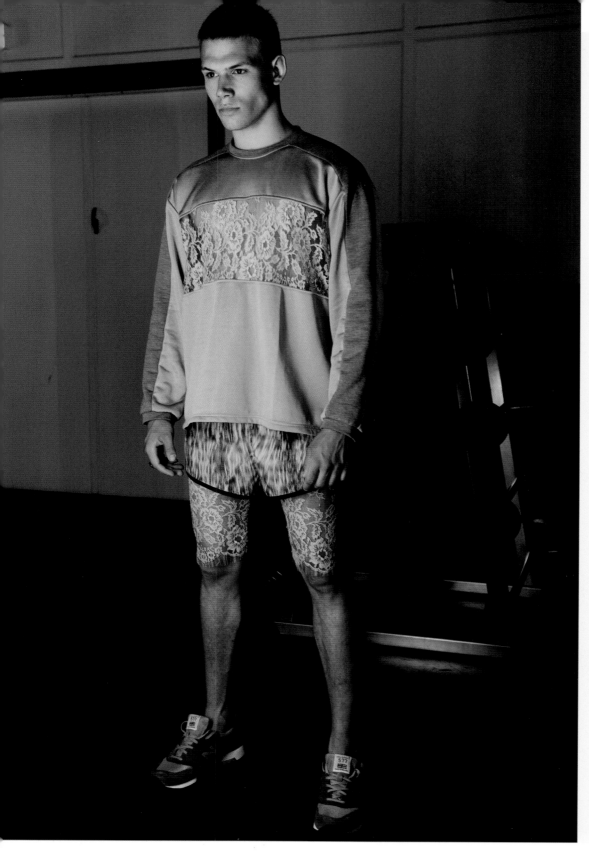

Page 246:
Astrid Andersen

Page 247:
Autumn Winter 2011-12
Image courtesy of Astrid Andersen

On these pages:
Spring Summer 2012
All images courtesy of Astrid Andersen

On these pages:
Spring Summer 2012
All images courtesy of Astrid Andersen

MARTIN LAMOTHE

www.martinlamothe.es
BARCELONA
Spain

Elena Martín is the artistic director and head designer of Martin Lamothe. She also teaches design, fashion, art direction, styling and gives master's degrees at several universities in Spain and México. Elena combines all this with her activity as a freelance coolhunter, doing market research for companies in Spain and the United States, and at the same time she designs for international brands as a freelancer.

After her graduation in Barcelona, she won the European contest Filatti Pitti, in Florence. Elena moved to London, with only 21 years old, where she graduated in the prestigious Central Saint Martins College of Art and Design. Once in London shre worked as an assistant for Vivienne Westwood and Alexander McQueen for two years. The third year she worked as fashion stylist for music world celebrities such as Kylie Minogue, Cher and Howie B, winning several awards.

Back in Barcelona in 2004, when she was only 25, Elena was selected to manage the design direction in Miró Jeans, the denim brand of the Catalan designer Antonio Miró. She completed there four seasons and two shows in the Pasarela Gaudí with recognized success. In 2007 she started her own fashion label Martin Lamothe, presenting her first collections at the Bread & Butter, Barcelona and Berlin, and at the Rendez Vous during the Paris Fashion Week. The brand soon developed an international growth. Martin Lamothe is now a recognized vanguard brand with sales in Europe, America, Asia and the Middle East.

Elena Martín es la directora artística y la diseñadora de la marca Martin Lamothe. También es docente de diseño, moda , dirección artística y estilismo en másters y graduados en varias universidades de España y de Méjico. Por si fuera poco lo combina con su actividad como coolhunter y haciendo estudios de mercado para empresas en España y Estados Unidos. También diseña como freelance para grandes marcas nacionales e internacionales.

Completó sus estudios de moda en Barcelona y ganó el Pitti Filatti de Florencia. Elena se traslada a Londres con tan sólo 21 años y se gradúa en la prestigiosa Central Saint Martins College of Art and Design. En Londres trabajará como asistente de Vivienne Westwood y Alexander McQueen, durante dos años. Durante el tercer año de su aventura londinense trabajó como estilista de estrellas del mundo de la música como Kylie Minogue, Cher o Howie B.

En el 2004 y con tan sólo 25 años le ofrecen la dirección de diseño de la marca Miró Jeans, la línea denim de Antonio Miró. En Miró Jeans diseñó cuatro temporadas completas y dos desfiles en la Pasarela Gaudí con mucho éxito. En el año 2007 Elena crea su propia marca, de inclinación unisex, Martin Lamothe, y presenta sus primeras colecciones en el Bread & Butter de Barcelona y Berlín, y en el Rendez Vous de París. Actualmente Martin Lamothe es una marca muy reconocida con ventas en Europa, América, Asia, Próximo Oriente y Arabia Saudí.

Page 252:
Elena Martín

Page 253:
Autumn Winter 2012-13
Image courtesy of Martin Lamothe

On these pages:
Paris, Texas
Autumn Winter 2009-10
Images courtesy of Martin Lamothe

On these pages:
Paris, Texas
Autumn Winter 2009-10
Images courtesy of Martin Lamothe

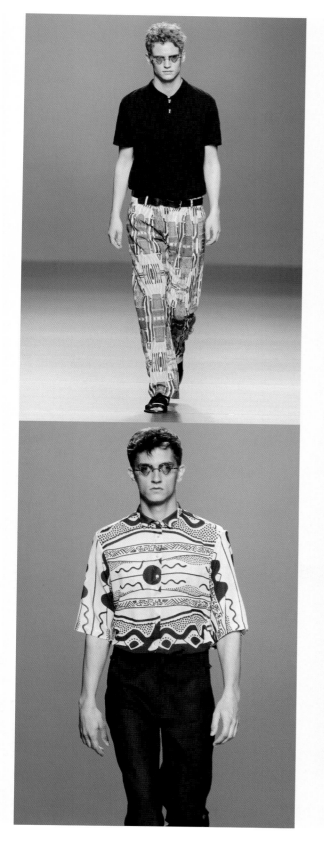

CARLOS DÍEZ DÍEZ

www.carlosdiezdiez.com
MADRID
Spain

Carlos Diez Diez was born in Bilbao, a city in which he studied design and industrial pattern making techniques. During the three-year career Carlos participates in several fashion contests winning first prize in each of the targets: menswear, womenswear and kids, earning a scholarship that will take him to the city of New York to complete his studies. After his graduation he moved to Madrid where he worked as an assistant for the famous Spanish fashion designer Antonio Alvarado, after that hew worked as fashion stylist for magazines, films and advertising.

In 2004 he launched his own label "Díez Díez", and since 2004 he presents his collections in the Pasarela Cibeles during the Madrid Fashion Week, winning countless awards. Carlos collaborates designing for other brands like Lois (Lois by Carlos Díez), Converse (Converse by Carlos Díez), Beefeater, Campari, Coca-Cola or Disney, and he also designs once a year an underwear collection for the brand Jockey.

In 2009, Carlos opened his own store and studio in Madrid from where he operates working on his own collections and collaborations for other brands. He also loves to work as a Dj in several clubs and festivals throughout the Spanish geography.

Carlos Díez Díez nace en Bilbao, ciudad en la que estudia diseño, patronaje industrial y técnicas de la confección. Durante los tres años de carrera participa en concursos de moda en los que obtiene el primer premio en cada una de las modalidades masculina, femenina e infantil y recibe una beca que le llevara a la ciudad de Nueva York para completar sus estudios. Tras graduarse se traslada a Madrid donde trabajará como asistente de Antonio Alvarado y como estilista de moda, cine y publicidad.

En el 2004 forma su propia marca "Díez Díez" con la que comienza a desfilar en la pasarela Cibeles Madrid Fashion Week desde el año 2004 hasta la actualidad, ganando infinidad de premios. Carlos colabora diseñando para marcas como Lois (Lois by Carlos Díez), Converse (Converse by Carlos Díez), Beefeater, Campari, Coca-Cola o Disney y diseña una colección anual de ropa interior para la marca Jockey.

En el 2009 inaugura su propia tienda estudio en el centro de Madrid desde donde dirige todas sus operaciones, sus propias colecciones o colaboraciones con otras marcas. En la actualidad compagina su trabajo como diseñador con el de Dj pinchando en diferentes clubes y fiestas por toda la geografía española.

Page 260:
Carlos Diez Diez by Marcos Rico

Page 261:
Insert Coin
Autumn Winter 2012-13
Image courtesy of Oscar Diez Diez

On these pages:
Leather Jacket Love Story
Autumn Winter 2011-12
All images courtesy of
Carlos Diez Diez

On these pages:
Leather Jacket Love Story
Autumn Winter 2011-12
All images courtesy of
Carlos Díez Díez

Page 266:
Illustration by
Carlos Díez Díez

Page 267:
Drunken Kiss
Spring Summer 2012
All images courtesy of
Carlos Díez Díez

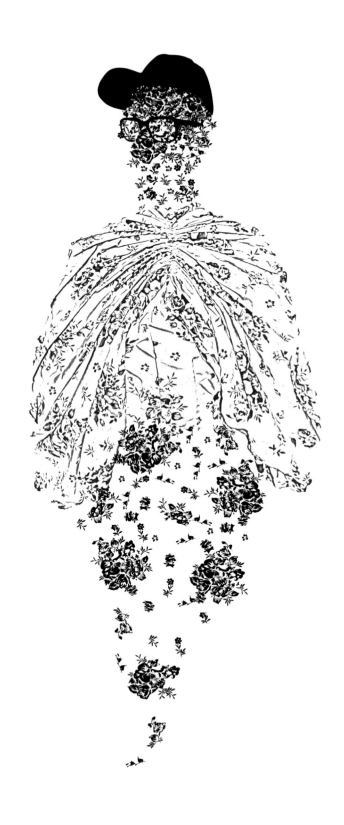

Page 267:
Drunken Kiss
Spring Summer 2012
All images courtesy of
Carlos Díez Díez

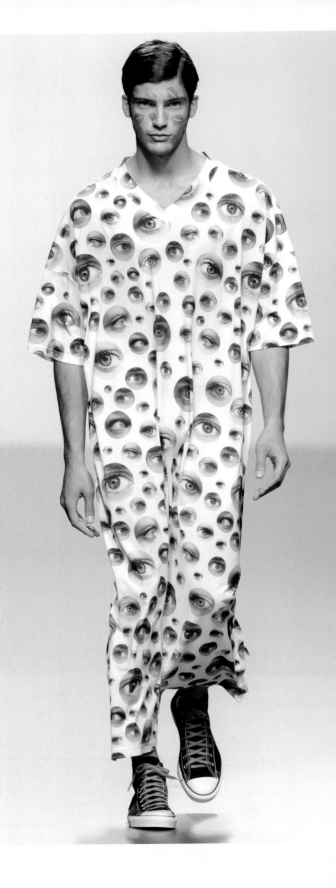

IXONE ELZO

www.ixoneelzo.com
GUIPÚZCOA
Spain

Ixone Elzo born in 1982 in Hondarribia, Spain. He studied fine arts at the Facultad de Bellas Artes in Leioa, finishing the final year in Ravenna, Italy, with an Erasmus scholarship. Shortly afterwards she studied a pedagogic skills course in the faculty of San Sebastian. After that Ixone decides to move to Barcelona where she graduated in fashion and textile design at the Instituto Europeo di Design. Her thesis project *Carne fresca* was selected in the 28th ModaFAD edition and was a finalist in the Project T, 2009. She presented her *Carne fresca* collection at the fashion week in Bogota, Colombia, 2009. Her next collection *Los restos del futuro* was a real success in ModaFad and once again in the fashion week in Bogota, in 2010, and in the 32-34N SOUTH 2010, in Cadiz. She also was finalist in the contest CREAMODA 2010 at the Bilbao Exhibition Center.

Finally Ixone Elzo debuts in 2012 at El Ego de Cibeles during the Madrid Fashion Week with the collection of *Trucha con lentejas*, becoming another promising young Spanish fashion designer.

Ixone Elzo nace en Hondarribia en 1982. Estudió bellas artes en la Facultad de Bellas Artes de Leioa, cursando el último año de la carrera en Ravenna, Italia, con una beca Erasmus. Poco después estudió Curso de aptitud pedagógica, en la facultad de San Sebastián, hasta que Ixone decide trasladarse a Barcelona donde se licencia en diseño de moda y textil en el Instituto Europeo di Design. Su proyecto de tesis *Carne fresca* fue seleccionado en la 28 edición del ModaFAD y quedó finalista en el Proyecto T, 2009. Presentó y desfiló con la colección *Carne fresca* en la semana de la moda de Bogotá, Colombia, 2009. Su siguiente colección *Los restos del futuro* fue todo un éxito en ModaFad y en la semana de la moda de Bogotá, en el 2010, y también en la edición del SOUTH 32-34N 2010, en Cádiz. Quedó Finalista en el certamen CREAMODA 2010 en el Bilbao Exhibition Center.

Finalmente Ixone Elzo debuta el 20 de septiembre del 2012 en el Ego Cibeles de Madrid con la colección *Trucha con lentejas*, convirtiéndose en otra de las jóvenes promesas del mundo de la moda española.

Page 270:
Ixone Elzo

Page 271:
Cabeza de Jabalí
Autumn Winter 2012-13
All images courtesy of
Ixone Elzo

On these pages:
Cabeza de Jabalí
Autumn Winter 2012-13
All images courtesy of
Ixone Elzo

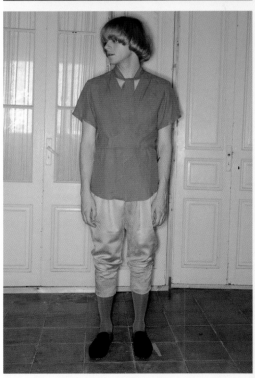

On these pages:
Trucha con lentejas
Spring Summer 2012
All images courtesy of
Ixone Elzo

On the following pages:
Trucha con lentejas
Spring Summer 2012
All images courtesy of
Ixone Elzo

BAARTMANS
& SIEGEL

www.baartmansandsiegel.com
LONDON
England

Baartmans and Siegel is a dynamic, luxury menswear label, that believes in creating interactive, innovative garments, and is currently shaping the landscape of contemporary menswear. The Dutch/English, London based, design duo met while at Viktor & Rolf, and were united in their belief of beautiful craftsmanship and imaginative design. The pair's work is fast becoming recognisable by their use of interactive texture and sharp tailoring. Self described as modern-traditionalists, Wouter Baartmans and Amber Siegel's work focuses on beautiful fabrics that seduce, and shapes that are accessible yet distinctive.

Both 2010 graduates of the prestigious Menswear Fashion Design and Technology BA and MA courses at London College of Fashion, Baartmans and Siegel showcase the best of British design, and already have the support of industry leaders, stylists, journalists and buyers. The Baartmans And Siegel brand is fast becoming one-to-watch: synonymous with interesting details and menacing masculinity. Their Autumn Winter 2011 collection is now available in Harrods. Baartmans and Siegel shall be showing their Spring Summer 2012 collection at London Fashion Week –with Vauxhall Fashion Scout's prestigious, 'Men's Ones To Watch Category', as part of the Men's day, as well as presenting with The British Fashion Council in the Portico Rooms.

Baartmans and Siegel es una marca dinámica de moda masculina de lujo, que diseña prendas interactivas e innovadoras dentro del paisaje de la moda masculina contemporánea. Este dúo de diseñadores, mitad holandés, mitad inglés, y con sede en Londres, se conocieron cuando los dos trabajaban para Viktor & Rolf, allí se dieron cuenta de que estaban unidos por su amor a la artesanía y al diseño imaginativo. El trabajo de esta pareja es rápidamente reconocible por el uso de texturas interactivas y por su modo de ver la sastrería. Wouter Baartmans y Amber Siegel se dejan seducir por tejidos y formas que sean accesibles y distintivas.

Ambos se graduaron en el año 2010 en el prestigioso Menswear Fashion Design and Technology y en el London College of Fashion, en Londres. La firma Baartmans y Siegel representan lo mejor del diseño británico, y ya cuentan con el apoyo de los líderes de la industria, estilistas de moda, periodistas de las revistas de moda más importantes y compradores a nivel internacional. Baartmans y Siegel se está convirtiendo en sinónimo de calidad, con unas prendas repletas de detalles interesantes y, según ellos mismos opinan, en un símbolo de la nueva masculinidad que nos "amenaza". Su ropa ya está disponible en las mejores tiendas, como por ejemplo Harrods y desfilan durante la London Fashion Week.

Page 278:
Wouter Baartmans and Amber Siegel

Page 279:
Dust Drifters
Photography: Amarpaul Kalirai

On these pages:
Dust Drifters
Spring Summer 2012
Photography: Amarpaul Kalirai

On these pages:
Milk Tray Man
Autumn Winter 2012-13
All images courtesy of
Baarmans & Siegel

Visit our official online store!
monsashop.com

Follow us on facebook!
facebook.com/monsa.publications